NATIONAL INCOME AND EXPENDITURE

NATIONAL INCOME AND EXPENDITURE

RICHARD and
GIOVANNA STONE

BOWES AND BOWES
LONDON

ISBN 0 370 00218 0
Printed in Great Britain for
Bowes & Bowes (Publishers) Ltd
9 Bow Street, London WC2E 7AL
by Ebenezer Baylis & Son Ltd
The Trinity Press, Worcester and London
Set in Monotype Times
Fifth edition of Meade & Stone's
National Income and Expenditure
rewritten 1961
Ninth Edition 1972

CONTENTS

INTRODUCTION

NATIONAL INCOME is a household phrase and in a general way what it means is obvious: it is the income of a nation as opposed to the income of an individual. But like many phrases in common use it may not have quite the same meaning to all who use it. If we probe more deeply and ask how it is defined, we shall have to clarify many concepts which are fundamental to the study of economics and to the conduct of business affairs. If we go further and ask how it is measured, we shall find ourselves surveying almost the whole field of economic statistics. When we reach the end we shall have outlined the anatomy of an economic system and obtained both a clear picture of the circular flow of economic activity and an essential tool for understanding many of the central problems of economic life.

Coming down to brass tacks, let us equip ourselves with a copy of the official Blue Book on *National Income and Expenditure* [61] which comes out each year in September. From small beginnings in the form of a White Paper issued with the Budget of 1941, this annual statement has grown to impressive dimensions and at first sight may appear too formidable and complicated to repay the attention of the uninitiated. But this is not so. True, the *Blue Book* does not waste any space on general explanations, but it sets out the main aspects of the nation's housekeeping in a fairly simple and straightforward way: by how much the total income of the community changes from year to year; how it originates in the various branches of production; in what proportions it is made up of wages, salaries, profits, interest and rent; how it flows into different channels of private and public expenditure; how that part of it which goes to individuals is spent by them on consumption, paid in taxes or saved; how that part which goes to public authorities gets allocated among defence, education, the health service and other purposes; how investment is distributed over different industries and different types of capital good; and so on. In short, the *Blue Book* provides the background for most reviews of the economic situation in Britain, such as appear annually in the *Economic Reports* [73], and it is around it and its American counterparts [81, 84], published by the U.S. Department of Commerce, that we shall work.

This short introduction to social accounting was written during 1960 in place of a fifth edition of Meade and Stone's *National Income and Expenditure* [34], which first appeared in 1944. Since social accounting hardly existed in 1944 and since the intervening years had also seen a great improvement in the statistics of national income and expenditure, we decided, in agreement with Professor Meade, that the time had come to give up revising the original version and to write a new one which would reflect these developments. A ninth edition being now required, we have taken the opportunity to bring the figures as far as possible down to 1969. We have also added a chapter, the present Chapter III, by elaborating and extending what used to be in earlier editions the last section of Chapter II.

The plan of the book is as follows. Chapter I defines the national income and relates it to other totals of income and product. Chapter II describes the three basic forms of economic activity, production, consumption and accumulation, and relates them to one another following the principles of an accounting system. Chapter III introduces the concept of sectors, private and public, and traces the course of the national income from its origins in the various sectors through a succession of transfers to its final use by the various sectors. Chapter IV takes up the question of comparing totals of income and product over time. Chapter V goes further and discusses the problems of comparing income and product levels in different countries. Finally, Chapter VI gives an outline of the more advanced forms of economic description which follow rather easily once the ideas of income, product and expenditure are understood. A list of works cited is given at the end of the book and the entries in it are referred to in the text by numbers enclosed in square brackets.

Cambridge R. and G.S.
August 1971

CHAPTER I

WHAT IS THE NATIONAL INCOME?

1. *The National Income and Other Income Totals*

LET US begin by asking what the national income is. We all know, broadly, what we mean by an individual's income. He may receive it as a wage or a salary from his work, as a profit from his business, as rent from his property, as interest or dividends from his securities, as a pension or grant from the state or from a public fund. Is the national income merely the sum of the incomes of all the individuals in the community?

The answer is no. The total of individual incomes, including the income of non-profit-making institutions, which are considered as aggregates of individuals, is usually called *personal income*. To this the qualification 'before tax' is sometimes added to indicate that taxes on income have not been deducted.

If we take the 1970 *Blue Book* [61] (to which we shall refer throughout) and look at table 2 we shall see that in 1969 total personal income amounted to £38,571 million. If we study the table we shall see that this figure relates to a concept of personal income which includes provisions for depreciation and stock appreciation. For the moment we shall not go into the meaning of these terms, but we shall see later that they are really out of place in a concept of income. At this stage we shall simply note that the figures for depreciation and for stock appreciation should be subtracted from personal income. They are not in table 2 of the *Blue Book* but can be obtained respectively from tables 58 and 67, and amounted in 1969 to £667 + 107 = 774 million. Thus personal income defined to exclude these items is £38,571 − 774 = 37,797 million. If we look again at table 2, we shall see that this total includes £99 million of taxes and net transfers paid abroad. An examination of tables 7 and 19 shows that this total is made up of £22 million of taxes and £253 million of transfers paid abroad *less* £176 million of transfers received from abroad. Accordingly, if we wished to define personal income to include transfers received from abroad, we should have to increase the figure of £37,797 million by £176 million, obtaining a new total of £37,973 million. Here, however, we shall define personal income as this total *less* all taxes and transfers paid abroad, which works out to £37,973 − 253 − 22 = 37,698 million. We do this for reasons of convenience, not for reasons of principle: when we come to section 3 of Chapter III, we shall find that this total fits naturally into the cycle of redistributions there described and we have wished to avoid the proliferation of minor variants of the main concepts we are using.

Let us now return to our quest of the national income. Starting from the readily intelligible total of personal income we shall note, in the first place, that some elements of income never get distributed to individuals at all. The most important of these is the *undistributed income* of business corporations. These corporations make a profit and sometimes supplement it with income from other sources, but only a part of it all is distributed to the shareholders; the undistributed part is retained by the corporations and, after deduction of income and profits taxes, saved for the extension of their capital equipment or for building up their reserves of securities and cash.

If we begin by restricting corporations to *private* corporations (or companies, as they are called in the *Blue Book*), the sum of their undistributed income and of personal income gives a total of *private income*, again before tax. An estimate of this undistributed income can be obtained from tables 26, 58 and 67 of the *Blue Book*. From table 26 we take the balance, undistributed income after taxation, and add to it British taxes on income (other than taxes levied on profits due abroad, which can be thought of as paid by the rest of the world out of the profits before tax that they receive), and additions to dividend reserves. This gives us a total for 1969 of £2,511 + 1,534 + 48 = 4,093 million. As with personal income, this figure includes depreciation (except for companies operating abroad) and stock appreciation. Tables 58 and 67 show that the necessary deductions amount to £1,412 + 704 = 2,116 million. The undistributed income of companies in 1969 after these deductions was therefore £4,093 − 2,116 = 1,977 million, and so total private income was £37,698 + 1,977 = 39,675 million.

To this estimate of total private income we must now add the undistributed income of *public* corporations and any other income which accrues to the state from its productive activity and from the property it owns. Let us take these additional items one at a time. From tables 32, 58 and 67 of the *Blue Book* we can see that in 1969 the undistributed income of public corporations (before tax and including additions to interest reserves, but deducting depreciation and stock appreciation) amounted to £890 − 1,094 − 4 = –208 million. From tables 43, 58 and 67 we can see that the trading and property income of the central government and local authorities amounted in the same year to £1,882 − 521 − 0 = 1,361 million. Thus the income from productive activity accruing to public agencies of all kinds amounted in all to £–208 + 1,361 = 1,153 million. If we add this sum to the £39,675 million of private income, we reach yet another income total, £40,828 million.

Is that at last the national income? The answer is again no, because the national income is defined as the sum of all the incomes accruing to the inhabitants of a country, whether as wages, salaries, profits, interest or rent, from their contribution to production, and from this alone. So far we have not bothered to make a clear distinction between income derived from *productive activity* and income derived from *transfers* (or redistributions of income). But this distinction is fundamental because, as we shall see, the sum of all incomes earned in productive activity is precisely equal to the value of all products emerging from the productive system. One pound earned in wages by a man working in a motor-car factory or in dividends by a man who has contributed his capital to setting up the factory corresponds to a pound's worth of motor-car. If then the workmen or the shareholder gives his pound to his godchild as a present, or to the state as a tax, and the state then perhaps passes it on to an old age pensioner, all that happens is that that bit of the country's total product is no longer enjoyed by the workman or the shareholder but by the child or the state or the old man. The value of the national product remains what it was before these transfers.

So the last step in reaching an estimate of the national income is to ensure that the income totals derived so far are free of transfer elements. In general there is no difficulty about this, but the details require a little care.

First, consider personal income. Gifts between persons, which are a form of transfer, are already cancelled out and do not appear in the *Blue Book*. The £35 million of transfers from companies to charities shown in tables 2 and 26 are paid out of the profits, rent and non-trading income of companies and so, since they are included in our estimate of personal income and are excluded from our estimate of the undistributed income of companies, no adjustment is needed. For the reasons already given, which will become clearer in Chapter III, we decided to exclude £77 million of transfers abroad (net) from personal income and so this sum must be added back. Finally, grants from public authorities, such as retirement pensions, sickness benefits, assistance grants and family allowances, must be deducted and these are shown in table 2 of the *Blue Book* to have amounted in 1969 to £3,930 million.

Second, there is another form of transfer which at first sight does not look like one. This is *consumers' debt interest*, of which the classical example is the interest paid by the government on the national debt. Why, it may be asked, should this be excluded from the national income? Surely if interest received from businesses is included, should not interest received from consumers, whether these be private individuals or the government, be included too? The answer to this is no. If the proprietors of a business decided to borrow any additional money needed in their business instead of providing it from their own capital, then in future they will have to share the income yielded by their business with the people from whom they have borrowed, so that their profits will be diminished by the amount of interest they will have to pay; in other words, the income arising in the business in the form of interest and profits together is independent of the method of financing adopted. If we now apply these ideas to a consumer we see at once that, since consumption involves the using up and not the bringing forth of goods and services, no product and therefore no income from productive activity can arise in the course of consumption. Accordingly, consumers' debt interest must be treated as a transfer, or better still as positive income from productive activity to the lender which is matched by a corresponding reduction in the income from productive activity of the borrower, which is indeed how we shall treat it in section 1 of Chapter III. By either of these means the national income is made independent of past and present methods of financing consumers' expenditure in just the same way that it is automatically independent of methods of financing producers' expenditure.

In the *Blue Book* the estimates of income from rent, dividends and interest received by persons are given after deduction of certain interest payments made by persons, notably mortgage interest paid to building societies and interest on bank overdrafts. This treatment, which is the correct one, is not however uniform: interest on hire-purchase transactions, for instance, is not deducted, and as no figure is given for it in the *Blue Book* we must for the time being be content with an estimate of the national income slightly inflated by it. As to the debt interest paid by the central government and local authorities, this is shown separately in table 43 of the *Blue Book* and amounted in 1969 to £1,898 million.

Third, in the *Blue Book* property income and taxes received from abroad are treated equivalently and so are the corresponding items when paid abroad. Thus the net property income from abroad, shown for 1969 as £451 million in table 1 of the *Blue Book*, can be seen from table 7 to be made up of £2,092 + 6 + 166 – 1,013 – 800 million. In our discussion of the undistributed income of companies before tax, we decided to exclude the £166 million of British taxes levied on profits due abroad; and we have nowhere included the £6 million of British taxes paid by non-residents on portfolio income. The sum of these items, £172 million, must now be added in.

If we make all these adjustments to our total of private income *plus* the income from productive activity accruing to public agencies, we obtain £40,828 + 77 – 3,930 – 1,898 + 172 = 35,249 million.

This is in principle the *national income*. In practice, however, there is one small hurdle still to be surmounted. The estimates in the *Blue Book* are made from a large number of sources and some of the figures relate to incomes while others relate to expenditures. When they are finally brought together they do not exactly agree. As a consequence there is a small *residual error*, or statistical discrepancy, and by convention the compilers add this when positive to the sum of their direct estimates of total income and subtract it when negative. In 1969 this discrepancy was negative, –£342 million. The final figure for the national income in 1969 is therefore £35,249 – 342 = 34,907 million.

Summing up, the national income is the income which accrues to the inhabitants, or normal residents, of a country from their participation in world production. All such income is included, whether it is received by individuals in the form of wages, dividends, interest, etc., or is retained in private businesses, or accrues to government bodies as a consequence of their business activities. No other income is included; therefore gifts, grants and benefits, which are not received for participation in production, are excluded and so is consumers' debt interest. It does not matter where the income comes from:

most of it will arise from production taking place within the country concerned, but some will arise abroad and will flow back to those who have provided the capital for undertakings abroad. In a corresponding way some of the income arising from production in the country will flow abroad to foreign shareholders, and so is excluded from the national income.

For many purposes, however, we need an income total which corresponds to the income arising from the productive activity that takes place within the territorial boundaries of a country, whether it accrues to the inhabitants of that country or not. Such a total is called *domestic income* and is obtained from the national income by subtracting *income from productive activity received from abroad* and adding *income from productive activity paid abroad.* According to table 7 of the *Blue Book*, in 1969 income (and taxes on income) received from abroad amounted to £2,264 million, and income (and taxes on income) paid abroad amounted to £1,813 million. Thus in 1969 the domestic income, as derived from the *Blue Book*, amounted to £34,907 − 2,264 + 1,813 = 34,456 million.

2. *The Net Domestic Product and Other Product Totals*

Domestic income is thus the sum of the incomes arising from the productive activity that takes place in a country, including the incomes distributed to foreigners in respect of their contribution to that activity. It provides a basis for valuing the production of a country and when considered from this point of view is called *domestic product* qualified as *net* and *at factor cost.* Let us see what these qualifications mean, and also what the reasons are for identifying income with product.

Goods and services have no abstract money value in themselves. We do not pay nature for accumulating large deposits of coal in the earth, or for stimulating the growth of pearls inside oysters, or for creating the human brain. When we speak therefore of the value of a good or of a service we mean the price we have to pay to induce human beings to bring forth these products for the enjoyment and enrichment of the community: the price we have to pay to induce, let us say, the miner to dig the coal out, the owner of capital to finance the necessary equipment, the owner of the land to allow his field to be dug up. Coal underground is worth nothing *per se*; nor for that matter is the pearl in the oyster or the latent ability of the poet or scientist. In order to bring into circulation these gifts of nature we need labour, capital and land. These are the three *factors of production.* Their contributions to production are called *primary inputs* and it is the rewards they receive for these inputs that constitute the first step in valuing what they produce. The sum of these rewards is the domestic income and it should now be clear why this is identical with the net domestic product at factor cost and why it is the fundamental valuation of what is produced in each country.

In producing goods and services, however, other expenses are incurred besides paying the factors of production. The *fixed assets*, such as buildings, ships and industrial equipment, needed for production are not everlasting and must be constantly renewed to keep production running steadily. The cost of these requirements is difficult to calculate exactly and the usual practice is to estimate it and set aside whatever sum seems likely to cover it. These provisions for the consumption of fixed assets are designed specifically to cover the wear and tear, in business language called depreciation, of capital equipment, its prospective obsolescence and any accidental damage to it. Commonly they go under the name of 'capital consumption' or of 'depreciation etc.', depreciation in the narrow sense of the word being by far their largest component, but in this book we shall refer to them simply as *depreciation*, dropping the 'etc.', and using the term in its general sense of loss of value. To get the full cost of products we must add depreciation to the incomes of the factors of production. We can see from table 1 of the *Blue Book* that depreciation in 1969 amounted to £3,694 million. If we add this to the net domestic product at factor cost we get £34,456 + 3,694 = 38,150 million, which is the *gross domestic product at factor cost.*

Are goods and services then sold at gross factor cost? The answer is no, because there are other elements that affect their value and consequently affect their *market price*; these are *indirect taxes* and *subsidies*. When we buy a packet of cigarettes for 30p about one third of the price goes in factor costs and depreciation and two thirds goes to the government in indirect taxes. Conversely, when a miller buys a ton of wheat from a farmer at the market value of £25 that wheat may well have cost the farmer £30 to produce but he will not lose money by selling it below cost because the extra £5 will have been provided by the government in the form of a subsidy. Thus if we add indirect taxes to a product total valued at factor cost and subtract subsidies from it we obtain the corresponding total valued at market prices. Again from table 1 of the *Blue Book* we see that indirect taxes, or 'taxes on expenditure', amounted in 1969 to £7,868 million and subsidies to £844 million, which gives us a balance of £7,868 − 844 = 7,024 million, called *indirect taxes* (*net*). If we add this to the gross domestic product at factor cost we get a total of £38,150 + 7,024 = 45,174 million which is the *gross domestic product at market prices*, or simply the *gross domestic product.*

Does this mean that in 1969 the British productive system turned out goods and services to the market value of £45,174 million? Superficially the answer is yes, but if we think over what we have said about depreciation we shall see that in fact it is no. The *final product* of a country falls into two main categories: those products which the community enjoys directly and uses up fairly quickly, namely consumption goods, and those more durable products which go to increase the capital wealth of the community, namely fixed assets, or investment goods. At first sight all new investment goods might appear to be an addition to the country's wealth, but we must not forget that in the course of producing both these and the consumption goods some of the existing capital equipment has worn out.

Thus part of the fixed assets produced in a period should be considered as a replacement of those that have worn out during that same period; not a physical replacement, ship for ship, factory for factory, but a financial one, the value of the new assets making up for the deterioration of the old ones. Therefore to get a true, or net, measure of what a country has produced we must deduct depreciation from the gross domestic product. This will leave us with a total of final product, valued at market prices, composed only of consumption goods and of that part of investment goods which has actually increased the existing stock of assets, namely *net investment* or 'additions to wealth'. The sum of consumption goods and net investment is the *net domestic product at market prices.* We have seen that in 1969 depreciation amounted to £3,694 million, and so the net domestic product at market prices for that year was £45,174 − 3,694 = 41,480 million.

The net domestic product at factor cost states the value of final product from the point of view of the producer. The net domestic product at market prices states it from the point of view of the buyer. The two gross product totals, at factor cost and at market prices, by including depreciation introduce among final product what is in fact a running expense and therefore an irrelevant element which belongs among the means of production, not among its ends. In principle, therefore, gross totals do not provide a true measure of product. In practice, however, they are more widely used than net ones because they are easier to calulate, as they avoid the tricky problem of measuring depreciation accurately. And since depreciation appears to be a fairly constant proportion of total product, gross totals are not too misleading for comparative purposes.

Having examined the meaning of these various product totals, let us now approach them by another route. If we think of the total production of a country, we think in the first place of all the products brought into being in that country over a certain interval of time, say a year. Some of these, such as raw materials, semi-finished products, fuels and business services, will be used in production. Others will be used by consumers, though they may be the same products, for instance coal, as are used by producers. Yet others, the fixed assets, will be accumulated and put to productive use in the future.

If we took every product produced in a year, valued it at its market price and added up the resulting sums of money, we should obtain a total which might be regarded as a measure of the total value of production in the country. But this measure would be an unsatisfactory one because it would involve a large amount of duplication. For example, coal and iron are needed to make steel and therefore if we included in a country's total product both the value of the coal and iron used in the steel industry and the value of the steel produced, we should find that we had duplicated the value of that coal and iron, since their value is included in that of the steel they have contributed to produce. So, to avoid duplication, we must subtract the value of the *intermediate products* used in steel-making from the value of the steel produced. The difference between these two values is termed *value added* in steel-making, and the sum of the values added in each industry will give us a total of final product free of the duplication of intermediate product.

Let us now see what happens to value added. Most of it, in the form of wages, salaries, profits, interest and rent, goes to the factors of production as a reward for their primary inputs; a smaller part goes to the government in indirect taxes; and the remainder goes to provide for depreciation.

Thus we see that total value added is nothing but the gross domestic product. We know that it is a total free of duplication as far as intermediate products are concerned. But if we want a total free of all duplication, in the same way as we have subtracted the value of the current goods used up in production we should subtract the value of the capital goods used up for the same purpose; in other words, we should subtract depreciation. By subtracting depreciation from value added we get the net domestic product at market prices. Finally, if from this we subtract indirect taxes (net) we are left with that part of value added which is distributed among the factors of production. This is simply the net domestic product at factor cost.

So much for the domestic product. Many people prefer another definition of product, which excludes income paid abroad and includes income received from abroad. This is a national as opposed to a domestic concept and, as we have said, gives a measure of a country's productive activity irrespective of whether this activity takes place at home or abroad. When calculated to exclude depreciation and indirect taxes it is called the *net national product at factor cost* and is numerically identical with the national income; as in the case of domestic income and domestic product, it is simply a way of looking at the same total from a different point of view. If to this total we add depreciation we obtain the *gross national product at factor cost* (termed in the *Blue Book* 'gross national product' without other qualification). If to this we then add indirect taxes (net) we obtain the *gross national product at market prices* and this is the total which we, in accordance with the more widespread convention, shall call for short the *gross national product*. Calculated in this way, the gross national product in 1969 was £34,907 + 3,694 + 7,024 = 45,625 million. Alternatively, we can pass direct to it from the gross domestic product by adding to the latter income from productive activity received from abroad net of similar income paid abroad. This will give us a total of £45,174 + 451 = 45,625 million, as before.

Although the gross national product is the most widely used of product totals it should be approached with great circumspection. First, it has the defect of gross concepts, that it embodies under the form of depreciation a number of products which should be classed as running expenses. Second, it has the defect of national concepts when applied to product, that it cannot be identified with a collection of complete products: if a motor-car is produced in Britain by the co-operation of British labour and foreign capital, its value will be the sum of the incomes which the British landowner, the British workman and the foreign investor derive from its production, plus indirect taxes and depreciation, so that by excluding that part of income which goes to the foreign investor we are left with only part of the value of that motor-car; in the same way income from abroad will represent only a fraction of whatever product the British investor has contributed to produce abroad. Third, the gross national product only takes into account movements of income and does not make the corresponding adjustments for indirect taxes, subsidies and depreciation, and is therefore a hybrid total.

3. *Taxes in the Valuation of Income and Product*

It is now time we discussed the position of taxes in these concepts of income and product. Why, it may be asked, having defined domestic income as income from productive activity, did we exclude indirect taxes from it but did not exclude direct taxes? Before we answer this question let us name the more important taxes in each category. The principal indirect ones are: customs and excise duties on tobacco, drinks and petrol, protective import duties, purchase tax, motor licences, stamp duties and local rates. The principal direct ones levied on income are: income tax, surtax, profits tax and national insurance and health contributions.

As far as indirect taxes are concerned the list is self-explanatory: they must be excluded from domestic income because they represent a business cost which does not remunerate any input into the productive system. In order to make beer we need malt, hops, sugar, yeast and other intermediate products, we need the use of vats and other durable equipment whose cost is measured by depreciation, and we need labour, capital and land whose remuneration constitutes domestic income arising in brewing. But we do not need, except in a purely legal sense, excise receipts for beer duty. The domestic income is intended to measure the income of all who contribute to domestic production and therefore the cost, in terms of factor rewards, needed to make that production possible. Evidently indirect taxes have no place in such a concept, whose importance can be seen from the following numerical example.

In Britain in 1969 private consumers spent £2,417 million on clothing and £3,518 million on drinks and tobacco. Of these totals, £215 million and £1,993 million respectively represent indirect taxes. Thus the payments to the factors of production, plus the provisions for depreciation, plus the imports required to satisfy these two categories of consumers' demand were £2,202 million and £1,525 million respectively. In other words, the relative resources involved, namely domestic factors, use of existing equipment and imports, were about 3 to 2, not the 3 to 4 that market values might lead us to believe.

This is the normal case. The payment of indirect taxes buys nothing which the branch of production concerned wants and nothing that it needs except a receipt. When the taxes get into the hands of the government they will no doubt be wisely spent to the great advantage of the community; but this has little or nothing to do with production. There may be abnormal cases, though we are unable to give a specific example. Thus it might happen that the government owned all durable equipment and instead of charging interest and depreciation to the industries in which this equipment was employed simply levied sales taxes, which over industry as a whole met depreciation and interest charges and also provided some net revenue. If such an unbusinesslike arrangement does exist anywhere in the world then evidently it is desirable to reckon the interest and depreciation charges embodied in this levy, subtract them both from it and include interest in the domestic income. Only thus shall we know what the resources used up in production have been. In short, we must always try to go behind the words to the underlying economic realities.

We come now to the second question: why is domestic income defined before the deduction of direct taxes? The answer is that incomes before tax are the amounts which have to be paid to buy the services of the factors of production. It is to be expected that the relative use of these factors in any branch of industry will be decided with reference to their relative prices; it is irrelevant to the producer that the owners of the factors transfer to the tax collector part of the price he must pay for their services.

To sum up, it is useful to have a product concept which excludes indirect taxes because these in no way represent a service to the production into whose cost they enter. Equally it is useful to have an income concept which includes direct taxes because the inclusive concept reflects the actual costs of different factors of production. Domestic income meets exactly these requirements, and the national income is simply the participation of the inhabitants of a particular country in the domestic income of the whole world.

4. *Some Recent Statistics of Income and Product*

Let us now pause and consolidate the position we have reached by reviewing the course of the national income and of other totals of income and product over the last thirty years. This is done in table 1 below for this country and for the United States of America.

Some interesting information can be obtained from this table. For instance, in Britain the undistributed income of companies as a proportion of private income was in 1969 (as in 1938) 5 per cent as compared with 7 per cent in America. In the 1950's the proportion was higher in both countries and in Britain reached a figure of 12½ per cent in 1954. In both countries, government income from property was small, though in Britain it had reached a figure of 3 per cent of private income by 1969. In Britain, with its well-developed social services and comparatively large national debt, transfers were 14 per cent of private income in 1969 as against 8½ per cent in America. In Britain depreciation was 10½ per cent of domestic income in 1969 as against 10 per cent in America. In Britain

TABLE 1

The National Income and Other Totals of Income and Product

	United Kingdom £ *million*					United States* $ *milliard* (*billion*)				
	1938	1954	1959	1964	1969	1938	1954	1959	1964	1969
1. Personal income	**4,996**	**13,920**	**19,205**	**27,070**	**37,698**	**69·5**	**295·4**	**394·0**	**514·7**	**786·0**
plus Undistributed income of companies before tax ..	274	2,005	2,302	2,534	1,977	1·8	28·7	39·1	48·5	61·1
2. Private income	**5,270**	**15,925**	**21,507**	**29,604**	**39,675**	**71·2**	**324·1**	**433·1**	**563·2**	**847·1**
plus Government income from property	76	113	218	704	1,153	0·4	1·4	2·0	2·9	3·6
less Transfers	–530	–1,566	–2,377	–3,347	–5,579	–3·4	–19·9	–31·4	–42·6	–74·1
plus Residual error (Britain) ..	0	116	230	–134	–342	—	—	—	—	—
3. National income	**4,816**	**14,588**	**19,578**	**26,827**	**34,907**	**68·2**	**305·6**	**403·7**	**523·5**	**776·6**
plus Statistical discrepancy (America)	—	—	—	—	—	0·6	2·7	–0·8	–1·3	–4·7
less Income from abroad (net)	–192	–250	–260	–395	–451	–0·4	–1·6	–2·2	–4·0	–4·3
4. Domestic income (net domestic product at factor cost) ..	**4,624**	**14,338**	**19,318**	**26,432**	**34,456**	**68·4**	**306·7**	**400·8**	**518·2**	**767·7**
plus Depreciation	359	1,340	1,844	2,492	3,694	7·3	28·2	41·4	56·1	78·9
5. Gross domestic product at factor cost	**4,983**	**15,678**	**21,162**	**28,924**	**38,150**	**75·7**	**334·9**	**442·2**	**574·3**	**846·5**
plus Indirect taxes (net)	585	2,082	2,831	3,949	7,024	8·6	28·3	39·3	54·2	80·6
6. Gross domestic product ..	**5,568**	**17,760**	**23,993**	**32,873**	**45,174**	**84·3**	**363·2**	**481·5**	**628·5**	**927·1**
plus Income from abroad (net)	192	250	260	395	451	0·4	1·6	2·2	4·0	4·3
7. Gross national product ..	**5,760**	**18,010**	**24,253**	**33,268**	**45,625**	**84·7**	**364·8**	**483·7**	**632·4**	**931·4**

* Components do not always add up to totals because of rounding-off errors.

indirect taxes (net) were 15½ per cent of gross domestic product in 1969 as against 8½ per cent in America.

If we look at the trends of the series in the two countries, the impression is that all the main totals have risen through time, the rise between 1938 and 1954 being particularly striking in America. But in making these comparisons we must remember that the estimates for different years are expressed in terms of the prices ruling at the time and not in terms of a fixed set of prices. In other words, while these money totals have been rising the value of money has been falling, and it is only if a money total has risen faster than the value of money has fallen that the corresponding total has risen in *real terms*. We shall come back to this problem in Chapter IV.

If we try to compare the figures for the two countries, we run into a similar problem: the British estimates are expressed in pounds, the American in dollars. To make a comparison we need to know the relative purchasing power of the dollar and of the pound. We also need to know the relative populations, since the comparison is most interesting when expressed as so much per head. At this stage we are not really in a position to make these calculations, but even so it is hard to resist doing sums on the back of an envelope. The population of America is roughly three and two thirds times as large as the population of Britain. In terms of purchasing power, the exchange rate of £1 = \$2·4 is usually believed to undervalue the pound; let us accept the common belief that £1 = \$3 is nearer the mark. If we multiply the population factor and the purchasing-power factor together, we get a factor of 11 with which to multiply the British national income in order to compare it with the American. If we take 1969, we see that 776·6/(11 × 34·907) = 2·0 approximately. This means that if national income per head at equivalent purchasing power is taken as a measure of the relative standard of living, then in 1969 the Americans were about twice as well off as the British. This is a crude comparison but we shall see in Chapter V that it is not very wide of the mark.

5. *The Sources of the Statistics*

In concluding this chapter a word is needed about the sources of the figures. In the case of Britain, their derivation from the 1970 *Blue Book* has been given step by step for 1969. Most of the figures for the other years can be derived in the same way from the same issue of the *Blue Book*. Some of the earlier figures, however, can only be derived from earlier issues, and therefore do not reflect certain minor changes in coverage and definition introduced in later issues. For 1938 some of the bits are missing even from the earlier *Blue Books* and had to be obtained from unofficial sources.

In the case of America, estimates for the years 1929 through 1965 are given in *The National Income and Product Accounts of the United States, 1929–1965: Statistical Tables* [84]. For later years, estimates are given in the national income issue of the *Survey of Current Business* [81], which normally appears in July. Each issue gives original estimates for the preceding year and revised estimates for the three years before that. Thus the figures for 1964 and 1969 given here are taken from the issues of [81] for July 1968 and July 1970 respectively.

Returning to table 1, the derivation of the American figures is as follows. To obtain personal income, item 1 in our table, we must take line 16 of table 1.9, or more simply 1.9.16, in [84], add to it 1.9.10 and 1.9.11 and subtract 2.1.25 and 2.1.26. Exactly similar calculations can be made from the *Survey* but here all references are given to [84] in which the lines of each table as well as the tables themselves are numbered. To obtain item 2 we must add 1.9.9 and subtract 1.9.14. To obtain item 3 we must add 3.3.32 (which unlike 3.1.30 we treat as a profit and not as an indirect tax), subtract 1.9.12 and 1.9.13 and add back 2.1.25 and 2.1.26. To obtain item 4 we must add 1.9.6 and subtract 1.12.80. To obtain item 5 we must add 1.9.2. To obtain item 6 we must add 1.9.4 and subtract 3.1.30. Finally, if to this total we add back 1.12.80 we obtain item 7, the gross national product, which is identical to 1.1.1 in [84].

As to the principles on which these official publications are compiled, the conceptual framework of the British national income statistics and an account of the sources and methods used in estimating them are set out in *National Income Statistics: Sources and Methods* [64], which appeared in 1956, and in a revised version, *National Accounts Statistics: Sources and Methods* [66], which appeared in 1968. For America, details of this kind are given in *National Income, 1954 Edition* [82], *U.S. Income and Output* [83] and the issue of the *Survey* for August 1965. Both countries produce a large number of quarterly statistics which enable the national income picture to be kept up to date: the British estimates appear in *Economic Trends* [60], the American ones in [81]. The British government also issues each year at the time of the Budget a White Paper entitled *Preliminary Estimates of National Income and Balance of Payments* [62].

CHAPTER II

FROM NATIONAL INCOME TO NATIONAL ACCOUNTS

1. *Forms of Economic Activity*

IN THE preceding chapter we have distinguished between a number of totals of income and product and shown how to pass from one to the other. The time has now come to define the constituents of these totals and show how they are related to each other to form a closed network of flows. In doing this we shall gain some insight into the basic structure of an economic system.

An economic system is one in which goods and services are produced with the ultimate object of satisfying human wants. *Production* takes place in mines, farms, factories, shops, offices and other workplaces and, as we have seen, the total product of any period can be divided into two parts, intermediate product and final product.

Final product in its turn is divided into two parts: the first and largest flows into *consumption*, that is to say it is bought by final buyers for use within the period. The second constitutes an addition to the wealth of the country: most of it goes to maintain and increase the fixed assets needed to produce more goods and services; the remainder consists of those products intended for intermediate or final consumption which have not in fact been consumed within the period and so form a reserve, called increase in stocks or investment in stocks, which will be available at the end of the period for use in the future. This addition to wealth, whether in the shape of fixed assets or of an increase in stocks, is called *accumulation*. Since the whole of final product is either consumed immediately or accumulated for the future, it follows that *final product equals consumption plus accumulation.*

Production, consumption and accumulation are the three basic forms of economic activity. Its ultimate aim is consumption, but since production requires the services of durable equipment it is necessary that this equipment should be maintained and increased if consumption is to be maintained and increased. If a large part of production is accumulated it is to be expected that the capacity to produce will rise so that in the future more products will be available for consumption. On the other hand, if no part of production is accumulated it is to be expected that the capacity to produce will remain constant, and if the stock of durable equipment is not even maintained, the capacity to produce will fall. In practice, of course, other forces, social, political, scientific or natural, may affect productive capacity, but other things being equal, the larger the part of final product devoted to accumulation the larger will be future consumption as compared with present consumption.

All that has just been said relates to a *closed economy*, that is to say an economic system which is entirely isolated from other such systems. The economies of actual countries are never isolated in this way and transactions with other economies have to be considered. Thus the production of a given country is supplemented by imported products, and all the final product of a country is not exhausted by domestic consumption and accumulation but in part flows abroad in the form of exports. To trace such flows we must record not only all transactions connecting production, consumption and accumulation in the country we are considering, but also all transactions which the *rest of the world* has with that country.

If we record in four statements, or accounts, the *incomings* and *outgoings* relating to a country's production, consumption, accumulation and foreign transactions, we shall find that we have drawn up a closed network of flows which shows the basic structure of an economic system and explains how most of the income and product totals of Chapter 1 fit into it. Only personal and private income will not emerge at once, and the reason is that these two totals relate not to the economy as a whole but to institutional subdivisions, or *sectors*, of it. Once we have got the main structure clear we shall go into the question of sectors.

2. *Regions and Boundaries*

Since we are dealing with the structure of a system, some readers may find a simple geometrical analogy illuminating. We shall see in the next section that the idea of the *production boundary* is important and also that, just as we may think of production as a region cut off from the other forms of activity and from the rest of the world by a boundary, so we can apply the same idea to consumption, accumulation and the rest of the world.

We can represent the economy of the world by a closed area, say the interior of a circle. If we now draw a circle inside this area, the original circle will be divided into two parts, an outer ring and the interior of the inner circle. Let the outer ring represent the rest of the world and the interior of the inner circle represent the domestic economy. If we draw a second boundary which divides the interior of the inner circle into two parts we may identify production with one of these parts. If we draw yet another boundary which connects the inner circle with the second boundary and divides the second of the two parts in two, we may identify one of the new regions with consumption and the other with accumulation. Thus we can construct diagram 1 below.

In the following four sections we shall be concerned with the flows over the boundaries in the interior of this closed area. These flows will be expressed in terms of money due to be paid or received and not in terms of the goods, securities, tax demands etc., which flow the other way. Thus, for instance, the sale of goods from production to consumption will be represented by a flow of money from consumption to produc-

DIAGRAM 1

Regions and Boundaries

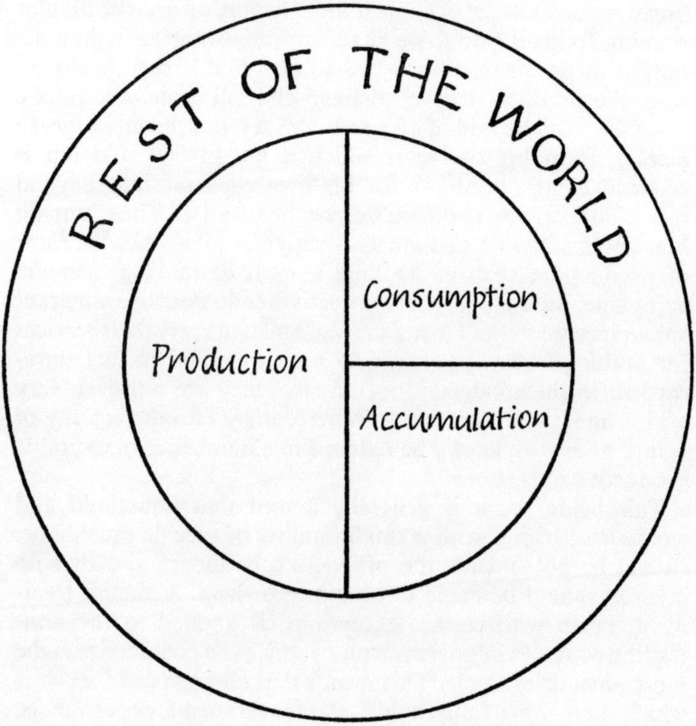

tion, although the goods themselves flow in the opposite direction.

3. *Production: Domestic Product Account*

What flows over the production boundary are the incomings and outgoings associated with bringing goods and services into being. Before we try to classify these flows let us consider what we include in production.

If we consider a business which makes cars or clothes or bread, or renders services such as transport or dry-cleaning or running football pools, we shall not only want to include its output in production but we shall also find it easy to do so, since the products are well defined and sell at definite prices. The same may be said of all goods and services *produced for the market*, including that part which is not in fact sold but is retained by the producer for his own consumption. Beyond this point, however, difficulties begin to arise. Thus, unpaid household activities and amateur activities often take the form of production, such as cooking a meal or making a model aeroplane. But in these cases the activities do not have a market value since household members and amateurs give their services for nothing; they are extremely numerous and in fact unrecorded; in the great majority of cases they are not even very well defined; and they merge imperceptibly into the activity of living, which can hardly be reduced to a number of measurable productive operations.

This being so, it is generally agreed that household and amateur activities, with a small number of specific exceptions, should be put outside the production boundary and that no attempt should be made to account for them. A similar treatment, again with certain exceptions, is applied to the non-trading activities of government, of which the civil service is the most obvious example. This means that all goods and services which flow into households and government departments, including the services of paid labour, form part of production, but that any further transformation they undergo inside households or government departments is not included in it.

This treatment is not a matter of principle but of convenience. Its acceptance rests on two grounds, one positive, one negative. The first is that the market economy, augmented by near-market activities such as those of the owner-occupier of a house and the farmer who withholds part of his product from the market for consumption by his family, is an interesting and useful object of study in itself. The second is that attempts to extend the production boundary by valuing household and amateur activities come up against an almost complete lack of information, so that the estimates that could at present be made would neither be useful in a study of the market economy nor make any real contribution to the study of domestic and government activity.

In advanced economies, where the use of money and the division of labour are highly developed and where business units are in most cases clearly separated from households, the concept of production just outlined is comparatively easy to follow. This is not so in primitive economies, where these distinctions are blurred. Since this book draws its illustrations mainly from two of the most advanced economies in the world no more will be said here on this subject. The problem, however, is one which greatly concerns the organizations engaged in setting up international standards for defining and measuring national income and product. On this and other questions the O.E.E.C.'s *Standardized System of National Accounts* [41] and the U.N.'s *System of National Accounts* [75, 76] and *Yearbook of National Accounts Statistics* [77] go far beyond this little introduction in matters of detail. In particular the U.N. publications, which try to standardize the national accounts of countries as diverse as the United States and Nigeria, have a good deal to say on a workable definition of the production boundary.

Let us now take a typical producer and enumerate the incomings and outgoings, or revenues and costs, connected with his production.

The main source of revenue is the sale of products. These sales may be made to: (i) other producers for purposes of current production; (ii) consumers, whether households, private non-profit institutions or departments of central and local government, for purposes of current use; (iii) other producers for purposes of maintaining or adding to their capital equipment; and (iv) the rest of the world. The first of these categories is intermediate product and the remaining three, identified respectively with consumption, accumulation and exports, are final product. Of course when the exports reach their destination they may be used in production abroad, but as far as the exporting country is concerned they leave its productive system and so are treated as final product.

A second source of revenue consists of the value of the increase in stocks: it may happen that more is produced in a period than is sold, in which case the stock of products in the hands of the producer, called *output stocks*, will be larger at the end of the period than it was at the beginning. And since, when we turn to the outgoing side of the account, we shall find the costs incurred in production charged whether the output has been sold or not, there must be on the incoming side of the account an imputed source of revenue corresponding to the value of any increase in output stocks.

The last source of revenue is subsidies, which in Britain are particularly important in agriculture, certain food industries and housing.

On the cost side there is first the intermediate product bought either from other domestic producers or from abroad. If, however, during a period more intermediate product is bought than is used up in production, this excess will represent an increase in *input stocks* which must appear also on the incoming side of the account as an imputed source of revenue, just like the increase in output stocks.

A second item of cost is depreciation. This, as we have seen, represents the value of fixed assets deemed to be used up in current production and is therefore a proper charge against the value of that production before the gain derived from it can be determined.

A third item of cost is indirect taxes, or taxes on sales. From the producer's point of view this too is a cost and, like any other cost, must be set against his sales revenue before his gain from production can be determined.

If at this point we strike a balance we shall find an excess of revenue over costs. This excess represents the gain from productive activity which is available for distribution among the factors of production. From the point of view of the owners of the business, however, part of this distribution of gain will represent further costs, such as wages to be paid to employees and interest to be paid to bond-holders. Only when these costs have been met do the owners of the business get the profit which accrues to them from their productive activity.

If we draw up an account on the above lines for every producer in a country and add all these accounts together, the sales and purchases of domestic intermediate product will be equal and so cancel out. Subsidies, instead of being considered as an item of revenue, are simply treated as a reduction in costs and subtracted from indirect taxes. Conversely, imports, instead of being considered as a cost, are treated as a reduction in the revenue from exports. This leaves us with a total of revenue consisting of the proceeds of final sales to domestic buyers *plus* the value of the increase in stocks *plus* net exports, which is equal to the gross domestic product; if depreciation is subtracted from this, there results the net domestic product at market prices; if indirect taxes (net) are subtracted from this second total, there results the net domestic product at factor cost or domestic income, which is either retained in the country or paid abroad.

These transactions are set out for Britain and America in table 2.

We can see from this table that between 1938 and 1969 the value of the gross domestic product increased eight times in Britain and eleven times in America. These increases in value, being largely due, as we have said, to higher price levels, do not reflect proportionate increases in quantities. We shall see in Chapter IV that, although the total product did increase in both countries, these increases were much smaller than the above figures suggest: just over 100 per cent in Britain and just under 280 per cent in America.

TABLE 2

Production
(Domestic Product Account)

	United Kingdom £ *million*					United States* $ *milliard* (*billion*)				
	1938	1954	1959	1964	1969	1938	1954	1959	1964	1969
1. Sales										
(*a*) Consumers (8)	5,166	15,276	20,118	26,971	36,736	74·6	299·8	392·1	509·4	671·7
(*b*) Capital purposes (13a) ..	656	2,552	3,736	5,857	7,927	9·7	64·8	86·7	108·7	159·3
(*c*) Abroad (net) (19)	–254	–124	–35	–604	217	0·9	0·2	–2·0	4·5	–2·3
2. Value of the increase in stocks (13b)	0	56	174	649	294	–0·9	–1·5	4·8	5·8	8·5
Total incomings	5,568	17,760	23,993	32,873	45,174	84·3	363·2	481·5	628·5	927·1
3. Depreciation (11)	359	1,340	1,844	2,492	3,694	7·3	28·2	41·4	56·1	78·9
4. Indirect taxes (net) (7)	585	2,082	2,831	3,949	7,024	8·6	28·3	39·3	54·2	80·6
5. Domestic income to										
(*a*) Domestic sectors† (6a) ..	4,563	13,754	18,412	25,257	32,643	68·2	306·3	400·3	517·2	764·0
(*b*) Abroad (16)	61	584	906	1,175	1,813	0·2	0·4	0·5	1·0	3·7
Total outgoings	5,568	17,760	23,993	32,873	45,174	84·3	363·2	481·5	628·5	927·1

* Components do not always add up to totals because of rounding-off errors.
† Includes residual error (Britain), statistical discrepancy (America).

Therefore, what with the changes in the value of money over the last thirty years and the different currencies used in the two countries, table 2 and the three which follow it are not very useful for comparisons over time and space except where these comparisons take the form of ratios within countries. For example, we can see from table 2 that in 1938 gross domestic investment in fixed assets (item 1b) was 12 per cent of gross domestic product in Britain and 11½ per cent in America. In 1969 the corresponding percentages were 17½ and 17. Thus in both countries the percentage was higher in 1969 than in 1938, and at each date it was slightly higher in Britain than in America.

But even this kind of comparison needs to be handled with care. First, there is the question of definition. In each country this has remained unchanged throughout the thirty years under review and the figures in a series are in principle comparable, although it should be remembered that the earlier ones, because of the insufficiency of statistical data, are likely to be less accurate than the later ones. But between the two countries comparability is more difficult to ensure, as the headings do not always cover the same categories. To take again item 1b as an example, the American definition of investment in fixed assets is different from ours, as we include in it public as well as private investment whereas the Americans restrict it to the private sector, bracketing public investment with other government purchases of goods and services. Accordingly, to make the series more comparable between the two countries we have transferred the one item of government investment shown separately in the American accounts, namely government expenditures on structures, from government purchases to investment.

Second, there is the question of what basis of valuation is used. All the totals in table 2, on which the above percentages are based, are expressed at market prices, which means that indirect taxes are included. For our present comparative purpose it is impossible to express them otherwise since the

Americans only give market-price values, but if these same totals were expressed at factor cost the relative position of consumption and investment as percentages of domestic product would be slightly different: indirect taxes fall more heavily on consumption goods than on investment goods, so that valued at market prices consumption appears relatively larger and investment relatively smaller than they are when valued at factor cost; also, as indirect taxes are lighter in America than in Britain, any excess of the British over the American percentage for investment appears smaller at market prices than it would at factor cost.

Third, there is the question of the changes over time in the relative prices of goods. While almost all prices have risen in the last thirty years, those of investment goods have on the whole risen rather more than those of consumption goods. Thus some part of the increase in the percentages between 1938 and 1969 is due to the fact that investment goods were relatively more expensive at the second date and not to the fact that relatively more of them were being bought.

Finally, the structure of values is different in the two countries. In America, for instance, investment goods are relatively cheaper than in Britain, so that if we priced the components of the British domestic product at American values we should find the percentage for investment slightly lower than it is at British values.

These comments are only intended here as a warning. In Chapters IV and V we shall see how actually to make these calculations over time and space at constant values.

Before concluding this section a word is needed about the sources of the figures. Those for Britain all come from tables 1 and 7 of the *Blue Book* and their derivation is simple. Item 1a is equal to consumers' expenditure *plus* public authorities' current expenditure on goods and services; item 1b corresponds to gross fixed capital formation at home; item 1c is equal to exports and re-exports of goods *plus* exports of services *less* imports of goods and *less* imports of services. Item 2 corresponds to the value of the physical increase in stocks and work in progress. Item 3 corresponds to capital consumption. Item 4 is equal to taxes on expenditure *less* subsidies. Item 5a can best be obtained by subtracting capital consumption and property income (and taxes) paid abroad from the gross domestic product at factor cost; and item 5b corresponds to property income (and taxes) paid abroad.

The figures for America are derived as follows. Item 1a is the sum of 1.1.2 and 1.1.20 in the *Survey*, *less* the sum of 3.1.22 and 3.3.27, government expenditures on structures, which the *Survey* includes among government purchases of goods and services but which we treat as part of capital expenditure; item 1b is equal to 1.1.7 *plus* the sum of 3.1.22 and 3.3.27; and item 1c is equal to 1.1.17 *less* 1.12.80, net receipts of factor income from abroad, which the *Survey* includes with net exports. Item 2 is the same as 1.1.14. Item 3 is the same as 1.9.2. Item 4 is equal to 1.9.4 *less* 3.1.30. Item 5 is equal in total to item 4 of table 1 above and is divided between income paid to domestic sectors, 5a, and income paid abroad, 5b, with the help of information not provided in the *Survey*.

4. *Consumption: Income and Outlay Account*

Let us now turn to the flows over the consumption boundary In the last section we have considered a country as a producer, setting out its accounts as a businessman would, with revenues and costs connected with production alone. In this section we shall consider it as a consumer, setting out its accounts as an individual would, that is showing where it gets its income from and how it disposes of it. In this form of account all the items which we have met in table 2 as costs for the producer are, with one single exception, sources of income for the consumer, in other words flow from production into consumption. The exception is the provisions for depreciation; these, being as we have seen a sum which the producer must set aside as a future source of finance for the replacement of his fixed assets, cannot be distributed as income to anybody but must flow from production directly into accumulation.

The main constituent of consumers' income is the income which accrues to a country from its productive activity at home and abroad, in other words the national income. In addition to this there is some income from indirect taxes, which is reckoned as usual net of subsidies.

And how does a country dispose of its income? Most of it is spent on buying goods and services. This is *consumers' expenditure*, an outgoing which flows directly into production; indeed we have met it in table 2 as the producer's biggest source of revenue.

A second and much smaller outgoing flows out to the rest of the world in the form of private remittances and government grants abroad, or *current transfers abroad*; these are shown net, that is after deduction of all similar remittances and grants received from abroad. It will be remembered that in table 1 we treated transfers of this kind as deductions from income rather than as part of expenditure. Transfers, which are gifts, must not be confused with expenditure abroad, which consists of purchases of goods and services in foreign countries; these purchases abroad are treated for reasons of convenience as imports and are included, together with most other imports, in consumers' expenditure at home and thus find their way to the rest of the world through the production account.

The third and last item of consumers' outlay is *saving*, which is the excess of consumers' income over their expenditure and their transfers abroad. Saving flows from consumption into accumulation where it becomes, like provisions for depreciation, a source of finance for capital expenditure; it is important however to keep a clear distinction between provisions for depreciation, whose function is simply to maintain the country's wealth of fixed assets, and saving, whose function is to increase it.

In this way we obtain table 3, which relates to the income and outlay of Britain and America.

TABLE 3

Consumption
(Income and Outlay Account)

	United Kingdom £ *million*					United States* $ *milliard* (*billion*)				
	1938	1954	1959	1964	1969	1938	1954	1959	1964	1969
6. National income from										
(*a*) Domestic production† (5a)	4,563	13,754	18,412	25,257	32,643	68·2	306·3	400·3	517·2	764·0
(*b*) Abroad (20)	253	834	1,166	1,570	2,264	0·6	2·0	2·7	5·0	8·0
7. Indirect taxes (net) (4)	585	2,082	2,831	3,949	7,024	8·6	28·3	39·3	54·2	80·6
Total incomings	5,401	16,670	22,409	30,776	41,931	77·4	336·6	442·3	576·3	852·5
8. Consumers' expenditure (1a)	5,166	15,276	20,118	26,971	36,736	74·6	299·8	392·1	509·4	761·7
9. Current transfers abroad (net) (17a)	8	10	82	186	252	0·2	0·5	0·6	0·6	0·8
10. Saving† (12)	227	1,384	2,209	3,619	4,943	2·6	36·3	49·6	66·3	90·1
Total outgoings	5,401	16,670	22,409	30,776	41,931	77·4	336·6	442·3	576·3	852·5

* Components do not always add up to totals because of rounding-off errors.
† Includes residual error (Britain), statistical discrepancy (America).

The most striking feature in this table is the course of saving. In 1938, 4 per cent of income was saved in Britain and 3½ per cent in America; in 1969 the corresponding percentages were 12 in Britain and 10½ in America. This steep upward movement in both countries does not necessarily imply a change in people's attitudes to saving. Apart from government policy, the two main factors which influence saving are income and wealth, so that a change in the saving ratio is likely to be due, to a large extent, to a change in the relationship between these two factors. But the subject is a complicated one and we shall do no more here than refer to the treatment of it in [50, pp. 121–51].

The source of items 6a, 7 and 8 have already been given. For Britain, items 6b and 9 come from table 7 of the *Blue Book*; and item 10 can most easily be obtained by taking the figure for total saving before providing for depreciation and stock appreciation in table 6, subtracting from it stock appreciation and adding the residual error, which are given lower down in the same table, and finally subtracting depreciation, which is given in table 58.

For America, item 6b was filled in with the help of information not provided in the *Survey*. It should be noted that although items 5b, factor incomes paid abroad, and 6b, factor incomes received from abroad, are not shown separately in the *Survey*, their difference is given in 1.12.80, as we saw in the preceding section; it is this net figure which enabled us to pass from national to domestic concepts in table 1. Returning to the sources of table 3, items 9 is the same as 4.1.6 in the *Survey*; and item 10 can most easily be obtained as 5.1.11 *less* 1.9.2 *plus* the sum of 3.1.22 and 3.3.27 and *plus* 4.1.7, which we have treated as a capital, not as a current, transfer.

5. *Accumulation: Capital Transactions Account*

We come now to the flows over the accumulation boundary. These are all flows of capital. The incomings are two: depreciation, flowing in from production, and saving, flowing in from consumption.

The outgoings are three. First comes *domestic investment*, which is divided between expenditure on fixed assests (*less* sales of existing assets) and investment in stocks. Next comes *foreign investment*, or the net increase in claims against other countries. If we subtract depreciation from domestic investment we obtain net domestic investment, or the net addition to the country's tangible wealth at home; and if to this net total we add foreign investment we obtain the increase in the country's wealth at home and abroad. The third outgoing is *capital transfers abroad*, which are shown after subtraction of similar transfers received from abroad.

These flows are set out for Britain and America in table 4.

In a general way these concepts seem straightforward enough, but when we come to examining the estimates available we shall find that they present peculiar difficulties and are only now emerging from a distinctly unsatisfactory state. We shall illustrate this by discussing: (i) the definition of fixed assets; (ii) the treatment of durable goods not classified as fixed assets; (iii) the measurement of depreciation; and (iv) the distinction between investment in stocks and stock appreciation.

Fixed assets, as we have seen, are the durable goods used for the purposes of production. A factory and its machinery, a ship, a railway track, an office complete with furniture and typewriters, a fleet of taxis are all fixed assets. Natural resources become fixed assets from the moment they are put to productive use; thus a seam of coal or a piece of waste land are not fixed assets, but mines and cultivated fields are. Housing being defined as a productive activity, houses are fixed assets whether they are owned by a property company, a public authority, a private landlord or an owner-occupier. The purchase of fixed assets is charged against capital and is by far the biggest outgoing in a capital account; indeed it is the main object of accumulation.

But just as it is convenient to draw the production boundary

TABLE 4

Accumulation
(Capital Transactions Account)

	United Kingdom £ *million*					United States* $ *milliard (billion)*				
	1938	1954	1959	1964	1969	1938	1954	1959	1964	1969
11. Depreciation (3)	359	1,340	1,844	2,492	3,694	7·3	28·2	41·4	56·1	78·9
12. Saving† (10)	227	1,384	2,209	3,619	4,943	2·6	36·3	49·6	66·3	90·1
Total incomings	586	2,724	4,053	6,111	8,637	9·9	64·5	91·0	122·4	168·9
13 Domestic investment in										
(*a*) Fixed assets (1b)	656	2,552	3,736	5,857	7,927	9·7	64·8	86·7	108·7	159·3
(*b*) Stocks (2)	0	56	174	649	294	–0·9	–1·5	4·8	5·8	8·5
14. Investment abroad (net) (18) ..	–70	117	143	–395	416	1·1	–0·5	–2·3	5·7	–0·9
15. Capital transfers abroad (net) (17b)	0	–1	0	0	0	0·0	1·8	1·8	2·2	2·1
Total outgoings	586	2,724	4,053	6,111	8,637	9·9	64·5	91·0	122·4	168·9

* Components do not always add up to totals because of rounding-off errors.
† Includes residual error (Britain), statistical discrepancy (America).

to exclude certain productive activities, so has it been found convenient to draw the boundary round accumulation to exclude a certain number of durable goods: those bought for purposes which lie outside the production boundary, whose cost is included in consumers' expenditure, and those classified as replacement parts, which are treated as intermediate product.

Let us take the first category first. If we look at households and government departments we see that they own and use a large amount of durable equipment which does not contribute a revenue to production. Obvious examples of this are private cars and washing machines, which are consequently regarded as consumption goods. This is not a very satisfactory solution. And the problem becomes more difficult still in the case of public buildings, schools, roads, drainage systems and the like. Should we treat the purchase of such goods as current or capital expenditure, and if we are to draw the line somewhere, where should we draw it?

These questions are at the moment unsettled, but the tendency is, rightly, towards admitting more and more durable goods into the category of fixed assets. In Britain for instance, as we have seen, all capital goods acquired by public authorities, whether for productive purposes or not, are included in domestic investment, with estimates given for their depreciation. In America, on the other hand, they are treated as current expenditure together with all other government purchases, but a concession to their importance is made in so far as public works and buildings are concerned by giving a table which shows the composition of new public construction activity. In both countries, however, household durables, while kept distinct from non-durables, are included among consumption goods.

It would be much better to treat as fixed assets at least the major pieces of durable equipment bought by government and private consumers. The decision to do so, however, would involve more than just a revision of the boundary between consumption and accumulation. In terms of tables 3 and 4, having subtracted total expenditure on durable goods from consumers' expenditure (item 8) and added it to domestic investment in fixed assets (item 13a), it would then be necessary to divide it into two parts, one equivalent to the depreciation of existing durables, the other equivalent to consumers' net investment. The first could appear as a separate item of consumers' outlay, called perhaps 'consumers' depreciation', the second would be added to saving (item 10); and both would go to increase the incomings of the capital account (items 11 and 12) and thus balance the increase in domestic investment.

But this would be an extremely untidy and awkward solution because it would introduce some depreciation, whose place is among the costs of production, into the consumption account. To avoid this anomaly the boundary between consumption and production would have to be moved too, so as to recognize certain household and government activities as productive. This would admit all owners of durable goods into the production account, and the changes in tables 2, 3 and 4 would then be as follows. Total expenditure on consumers' durables would be switched in tables 3 and 4 from item 8 to item 13a, as above, and in table 2 from item 1a to item 1b. What we have called 'consumers' depreciation' would take its proper place in table 2 as an increase in item 3; at the same time, since it does represent that proportion of durable goods which has been consumed during the period, it would also be left as part of item 8 and would consequently be included in item 1a, thus balancing the increase in item 3. The value of consumers' net investment would be transferred to item 10, and so in table 4 items 11 and 12 would find themselves increased to match the increase in item 13a, as happened above.

Having recognized the owners of durable goods as producers and reallocated accordingly the money they spend on the purchase and depreciation of these goods, we now ask ourselves whether we have in fact accounted for all the costs incurred and the gains realized in using them. The answer is that we have where actual flows of money are concerned, but not where invisible costs and gains are concerned. When a man buys a car he thereby forgoes the income he would get if he invested that part of his capital in bonds or shares or other interest-bearing property. This means that running his own car costs him in current expenditure not only the price of petrol and repairs but also the equivalent of the income he forgoes. It also means that the enjoyment or the practical advantage he gets from his car must represent to him a gain equivalent at least to that income. So to get a complete picture of the function of durable goods in the economy we should not only bring out their capital value in the national accounts but also try to calculate the hidden costs and gains which derive from owning them, since these costs and gains obviously affect other branches of the economy, especially the service trades. The simplest way to do this would be to impute to the owners of durable goods, as is done for owner-occupiers of houses, an expenditure and an income equal to the interest on the capital value of those goods, reckoning this interest at the current rate. If this were done, items 1a and 5a of table 2 and items 6a and 8 of table 3 would be increased by the amount of the imputation.

Let us now turn to the second category of durable goods excluded from accumulation, namely replacement parts. Replacement parts may be individually extremely durable; nevertheless their cost, together with that of the labour needed to install them, is treated as a current expense and appears as an outgoing in the production account for the year in which they are bought, like intermediate product. This treatment is often extended to whole pieces of equipment such as typewriters, which in a large concern will be bought on a regular annual basis. Its justification is that the separate items of expense are small, numerous and not readily postponable, so that with minor variations in composition they tend to recur year by year.

In accounting terminology this is the renewals method of treating the maintenance of assets as opposed to the depreciation method. When it is employed, as it sometimes is, to the exclusion of depreciation it works well in normal circumstances but not in abnormal ones. A good example of this is the maintenance of the permanent way of railways. These works can be regarded as virtually everlasting provided they are regularly attended to. This maintenance expenditure is treated as a current cost of operating the railway and the problem of depreciating the permanent way does not arise. It may happen, however, that under the pressure of financial losses, say, or of a war the railway company is forced to put its maintenance service on an emergency basis and carry out only the repairs which are essential for immediate needs. If this is done without introducing into the production account some provision for the abnormal deterioration which will inevitably ensue, then the true cost of operating the railway during the emergency period is underestimated and its profit is correspondingly overestimated; also, the company's assets are represented in a misleading way since the track is in an abnormal state of disrepair and to put it right some extra expenditure of capital will be necessary in the future. Whereas if provisions for depreciation are introduced at the outset of the emergency, the true balance of costs and profits through time will be respected and the company will not find its capital resources strained when normal activity is resumed.

This brings us to the third question we undertook to examine, namely the measurement of depreciation. Three elements are necessary to calculate the depreciation of an asset: an estimate of its useful life, an estimate of the rate at which it will wear out and the price at which to value each successive stage of this wearing out.

Estimates of life can never be certain, if only because technical change may force replacement earlier than expected. However, a great deal of information is available about the life-span of different types of asset, so that in estimating the useful life of well-established types, past experience is quite a good guide. But with new types, where either the design or the materials or both have not been tested by use, the estimates can be little more than a guess.

Estimates of the rate at which assets wear out can be made in many different ways. The two methods most commonly followed are the straight-line method and the reducing-balance method. With the straight-line method, use is assumed to take place uniformly throughout the life of the asset, so that an asset whose life has been estimated at, say, ten years loses each year one-tenth of its full value. With the reducing-balance method a fixed proportion of the depreciated value of an asset is assumed to be used up in each period; thus if the proportion has been fixed at 20 per cent a year, then the asset loses 20 per cent of its value in the first year, 16 per cent (which is 20 per cent of its depreciated value) in the second year, 12·8 per cent in the third, and so on.

As to the price at which to value each successive stage in the depreciation of an asset, it is usual in private accounting to value it in terms of the original cost of the asset. This practice has the drawback that the prices of capital goods, as of everything else, are subject to change and in the last generation have tended fairly steadily upwards. Accordingly, a better estimate of the current cost of using an asset is reached if the depreciation of the year is valued not at original cost but at current, or replacement, cost. Thus if in a particular year the price of an asset whose life-span is estimated at ten years has risen by 50 per cent then, supposing the straight-line method to be applied, the depreciation charge for that year should not be 10 per cent but 15 per cent of the original cost, which is equal to 10 per cent of the replacement cost.

The important point to keep in mind about depreciation is that however it is calculated it can at best express no more than a reasonable expectation of the cost of using durable equipment. Events may turn out differently from what had been expected and in this case a capital gain or loss will be made. Often when a piece of equipment becomes obsolete before the end of its estimated life, the whole of the outstanding depreciation is charged in one lump against revenue in the production account for the year in which the asset was scrapped, so that it appears as a reduction in profits, whereas it is a capital loss and should be treated as such. Conversely, if a fully depreciated asset is still in use beyond the estimated time, it represents a capital gain and should not be treated, as it often is, as an increase in profits. These and all similar unpredictable gains and losses of capital should appear in the capital account. Unfortunately, with the data we have at present any record we could give of these fluctuations of value would be too incomplete to be significant, and so for the time being it seems wiser to leave them all out.

We come now to the fourth question on our list: the difference between investment in stocks and stock appreciation. Investment in stocks represents the increase that has taken place during the period in the quantity of stocks held by the productive system. In section 3 of this chapter we have seen that if production is greater than sales there will be an accumulation of output stocks, and if more materials are bought than are used in the period there will be an accumulation of input stocks. Also there will always be at the end of a period a certain amount of work in progress, which can be thought of as stocks of unfinished product. All these accumulated stocks will eventually become a source of revenue to production: the output stocks will be sold as they are, the input stocks will be transformed into finished product, the work in progress will be completed. Until they have actually been sold, however, this revenue can only be a notional one; what in fact happens is that some capital, instead of being invested in fixed assets, is tied up in holding these stocks of finished and unfinished product. This is why the value of the physical increase in stocks is also called investment in stocks and is represented as an outgoing in the capital account (table 4, item 13b) and an incoming in the production account (table 2, item 2).

But how is this physical increase to be estimated? If the opening value of stocks is subtracted from the closing value the difference will show the total increase that has taken place in the value of stocks during the period. This increase, however, may be due quite as much to an increase in the prices of the goods stocked as to an increase in their quantity, and is not therefore the figure we want. To get the required estimate we must take the increase in the quantity of each type of stock and multiply separately each increase by the average price fetched over the period by that particular kind of good. The sum of these products will give us the value of the increase in stocks. It may happen that in a period the quantity of stocks has fallen instead of rising, in which case investment in stocks will appear as a negative figure.

Stock appreciation, on the other hand, reflects the increase, also either positive or negative, that has taken place during the period in the prices of the goods held in stock. The simplest way of calculating it is to subtract investment in stocks from the total increase in the value of stocks. This will give us a figure for stock appreciation reckoned at the average prices of the period.

If positive, stock appreciation is a capital gain, if negative, a capital loss; in either case its place is among capital transactions and not among sources of income. We have excluded it altogether because, as we said above, it seems pointless to introduce in our accounts one comparatively unimportant item of capital appreciation when we cannot introduce any of the others. In the *Blue Book* stock appreciation is included in income from property, but it can easily be removed since a separate figure is given for it immediately below that for domestic income in table 1. In the *Survey* this subtraction is performed by the compilers by means of the 'inventory valuation adjustment'.

The sources for items 11, 12 and 13 have already been given. For Britain, item 14 corresponds to net investment abroad in table 7 of the *Blue Book*, and item 15 is obtained from the same table by adding together capital grants from overseas governments (net) and other capital transfers from abroad. For America, item 14 is the same as 4.1.8 in the *Survey*, and item 15 is the same as 4.1.7.

TABLE 5

The Rest of the World
(Balance of Payments Account)

	United Kingdom £ *million*					United States* $ *milliard* (*billion*)				
	1938	1954	1959	1964	1969	1938	1954	1959	1964	1969
16. Income from British (American) production (5b)	61	584	906	1,175	1,813	0·2	0·4	0·5	1·0	3·7
17. Transfers from Britain (America)										
(*a*) Current (net) (9)	8	10	82	186	252	0·2	0·5	0·6	0·6	0·8
(*b*) Capital (net) (15)	0	–1	0	0	0	0·0	1·8	1·8	2·2	2·1
18. Borrowing from Britain (America) (net) (14)	–70	117	143	–395	416	1·1	–0·5	–2·3	5·7	–0·9
Total incomings	–1	710	1,131	966	2,481	1·5	2·2	0·7	9·5	5·6
19. Imports from Britain (America) (net) (1c)	–254	–124	–35	–604	217	0·9	0·2	–2·0	4·5	–2·3
20. Income from productive activity to Britain (America) (6b)	253	834	1,166	1,570	2,264	0·6	2·0	2·7	5·0	8·0
Total outgoings	–1	710	1,131	966	2,481	1·5	2·2	0·7	9·5	5·6

* Components do not always add up to totals because of rounding-off errors.

6. *The Rest of the World: Balance of Payments Account*

Table 5 facing brings together the transactions which Britain and America have with the rest of the world. In other words it is a condensed statement of the balances of payments of the two countries. Of course where Britain is concerned America is part of the rest of the world, and *vice versa*.

The entries in this table have all appeared in one or other of the three preceding ones, where they were presented from the point of view of the two countries concerned. Here they are seen from the point of view of the rest of the world, so that incomings and outgoings have their position reversed. The purpose of the table is not to set up a system of international accounts but merely to tie up the loose ends of tables 2, 3 and 4, hence the mixture of income flows and transfer flows and of current and capital transactions. The arrangement of the entries has been chosen for convenience in consolidating this table with the others, as we shall see in the next section.

7. *The National Accounts*

Tables 2, 3, 4 and 5 constitute a complete set of national accounts for Britain and America. Their essential unity is seen more easily if the figures for one country in one year are brought together on one page. This is done for Britain in 1969 in table 6 below.

This table shows the structure of an economic system reduced to its simplest terms. The only distinctions made are between production, consumption and accumulation and, in the treatment of income, between income from productive activity and income from transfers. Into this framework all transactions in the system can be fitted by further subdivisions of the accounts and entries. The statement is incomplete in only one respect: it relates only to flows and therefore, while it shows the additions to the country's wealth which have taken place during the period, it ignores the accumulated wealth which already existed at the opening of the period. In other words it does not contain a balance sheet. In Chapter VI we shall see what the functions of a balance sheet are and where information can be found about national and sector balance sheets.

The heading and the numbering of the entries in table 6 follow exactly those in the preceding four tables. Each item appears twice, with the number of the corresponding entry shown in brackets after the heading. Thus item 1a corresponds to item 8, item 1b corresponds to item 13a, and so on.

The accounts in a closed system like that presented in this table can be combined in many different ways, with interesting results. For instance, if we consolidate the accounts for consumption, accumulation and the rest of the world, that is to say if we turn them into one and strike out the common entries, namely income from productive activity abroad (items 6b and 20), current and capital transfers abroad (items 9 and 17a, and 15 and 17b), investment abroad (items 14 and 18) and saving (items 10 and 12), we obtain an account for the gross domestic product which is identical with the production account except that incomings and outgoings are reversed: what is a source of revenue inside the production boundary becomes an item of expenditure outside it, and what is a cost to production becomes a source of revenue either to consumption or to accumulation or to the rest of the world.

Similarly, if we consolidate the accounts for production and the rest of the world, items 1c and 19 will cancel out and so will items 5b and 16; and if we then consolidate the accounts for consumption and accumulation, item 12 will cancel item 10, and we shall have another pair of identical accounts with incomings and outgoings reversed. This pair will show the composition of the gross national product, consisting on one side of the national income *plus* indirect taxes (net) *plus* depreciation, and on the other side of consumers' expenditure *plus* investment at home and abroad *plus* current and capital transfers abroad.

These two examples illustrate the rule that if the accounts in

TABLE 6

National Accounts of the United Kingdom in 1969
(£ *million*)

Production
(Domestic Product Account)

1. Sales		3. Depreciation (11)	3,694
(*a*) Consumers (8)	36,736	4. Indirect taxes (net) (7) ..	7,024
(*b*) Capital purposes (13a)	7,927	5. Domestic income to ..	
(*c*) Abroad (net) (19) ..	217	(*a*) Domestic sectors* (6a)	32,643
2. Value of the increase in stocks (13b)	294	(*b*) Abroad (16)	1,813
Total incomings	45,174	Total outgoings	45,174

Consumption
(Income and Outlay Account)

6. National income from		8. Consumers' expenditure (1a)	36,736
(*a*) Domestic production* (5a)	32,643	9. Current transfers abroad (net) (17a)	252
(*b*) Abroad (20)	2,264	10. Saving* (12)	4,943
7. Indirect taxes (net) (4) ..	7,024		
Total incomings	41,931	Total outgoings	41,931

Accumulation
(Capital Transactions Account)

11. Depreciation (3)	3,694	13. Domestic investment in	
12. Saving* (10)	4,943	(*a*) Fixed assets (1b) ..	7,927
		(*b*) Stocks (2)	294
		14. Investment abroad (net) (18)	416
		15. Capital transfers abroad (net) (17b)	0
Total incomings	8,637	Total outgoings	8,637

The Rest of the World
(Balance of Payments Account)

16. Income from British production (5b)	1,813	19. Imports from Britain (net) (1c)	217
17. Transfers from Britain ..		20. Income from productive activity to Britain (6b) ..	2,264
(*a*) Current (net) (9) ..	252		
(*b*) Capital (net) (15) ..	0		
18. Borrowing from Britain (net) (14)	416		
Total incomings	2,481	Total outgoings	2,481

* Includes residual error.

a closed system are consolidated into two groups, the two resulting accounts will be mirror images of each other.

The totals thus obtained, however, may not always be so significant as the two we have reached in our examples. To get a worthwhile total it may sometimes be necessary to adopt a process slightly more complicated than simple consolidation. Let us suppose, for instance, that we want to find out how much the inhabitants of a country have consumed and how much they have added to their wealth. To this end, having chosen the accounts which look most appropriate, namely consumption and accumulation, we must first consolidate them; this will give us, as we have seen, the gross national product, composed on the outgoing side of consumers' expenditure (item 8) *plus* investment at home and abroad (items 13a, 13b and 14) *plus* transfers abroad (items 9 and 15). The next step is to get rid of these transfers, which is done by moving items 9 and 15 to the other side of the account, changing their signs. This will leave us with a total composed of consumers' expenditure and gross investment, so that the final step is to subtract depreciation from it; this is done by moving item 11 to the other side of the account, of course changing its sign. Thus we shall reach on the outgoing side a total composed of expenditure on consumption goods (item 8) and net investment (items 13a, 13b and 14 *less* item 11), and on the incoming side we shall have the flows of income which finance this consumption and this investment, namely the national income and indirect taxes, net of our gifts to foreigners (items 6a, 6b and 7 *less* items 9 and 15). The same results in reverse will be obtained by performing the corresponding operations on the accounts for production and the rest of the world.

By such means we can readily discover the identities between sets of transactions which follow from the system of definitions we have proposed.

CHAPTER III

SECTORS AND THE GENERATION, DISTRIBUTION AND USE OF INCOME

1. *Sectors*

THE *Blue Book* and the *Survey* contain a large number of detailed tables on which we have not touched and shall not touch in this little book. They all fit, however, into the framework we have developed and are obtained by taking the national accounts to pieces in different ways. Thus the domestic product account can be subdivided by industries, or by geographical regions or by legal forms of organization such as companies, unincorporated businesses, public corporations and so on.

These last subdivisions are the *sectors* of the economy. An important distinction is that between the private and the public sector, that is between individuals, non-profit institutions and private companies on the one hand and public corporations and the departments of central and local government on the other. As an example of how one of our tables can be expanded we shall now set out a consumption account for each of these two sectors.

Table 7 below gives the income and outlay of the private sector for Britain and America.

In this table we have taken the opportunity of including some additional details not shown in table 3. Thus that part of income from productive activity which represents the private sector's share of the national income is subdivided into three types of income, the last of which is in its turn divided between the amount received by persons (individuals, unincorporated businesses and non-profit-making institutions) and the

TABL

Income and Outla

	United Kingdo £ *million*		
	1938	1954	195
1. Income from productive activity†	**4,997**	**14,968**	**19,9**
(*a*) Income from employment	3,022	10,284	14,1
(*b*) Income from self-employment	613	1,384	1,6
(*c*) Interest (net), profits and rent			
(i) received by persons	1,088	1,295	1,8
(ii) retained by companies	274	2,005	2,3
2. Income from transfers	**273**	**957**	**1,5**
(*a*) Benefits and grants from the central government‡	250	924	1,5
(*b*) Benefits and grants from local government‡	25	20	
(*c*) Net transfers to persons from other sources	–2	13	
Total incomings	**5,270**	**15,925**	**21,5**
3. Consumers' expenditure	**4,394**	**12,091**	**16,1**
(*a*) Food	1,285	3,675	4,6
(*b*) Drink	285	794	9
(*c*) Tobacco	177	855	1,0
(*d*) Clothing	446	1,205	1,5
(*e*) Housing	518	1,056	1,5
(*f*) Major durable goods			
(i) household	..	603	8
(ii) vehicles	..	234	5
(*g*) Public transport	167	445	5
(*h*) All other	..	3,224	4,4
4. British (American) taxes on income	**489**	**2,563**	**3,5**
(*a*) Social security contributions	109	532	8
(*b*) Income tax and surtax paid by persons	292	1,236	1,7
(*c*) Income tax and profits taxes paid by companies	88	795	8
5. Saving†	**387**	**1,271**	**1,8**
(*a*) Persons	201	61	4
(*b*) Companies	186	1,210	1,4
Total outgoings	**5,270**	**15,925**	**21,5**

* Components do not always add up to totals because of rounding-off erro

† Does not include residual error or statistical discrepancy.

f the Private Sector

		United States* $ *milliard (billion)*				
1964	1969	1938	1954	1959	1964	1969
7,363	**35,809**	**68·6**	**308·5**	**407·1**	**527·1**	**782·8**
9,702	27,174	45·0	208·0	279·1	365·7	564·2
2,017	2,547	11·3	40·0	46·6	52·3	66·8
3,110	4,111	10·5	31·9	42·4	60·6	90·7
2,534	1,977	1·8	28·7	39·1	48·5	61·1
2,241	**3,866**	**2·7**	**15·5**	**26·0**	**36·1**	**64·3**
2,181	3,783	1·2	11·5	20·1	27·8	50·0
76	147	1·2	3·4	4·8	6·5	11·5
–16	–64	0·3	0·6	1·1	1·9	2·7
9,604	**39,675**	**71·2**	**324·1**	**433·1**	**563·2**	**847·1**
1,459	**28,618**	**63·9**	**236·5**	**311·2**	**401·2**	**577·5**
5,529	6,705	15·6	56·5	68·4	80·5	105·3
1,328	1,824	3·3	8·9	10·2	13·0	16·4
1,343	1,694	1·7	4·9	6·6	7·9	10·2
1,971	2,417	8·0	26·8	31·9	40·4	59·4
2,343	3,590	8·9	31·7	43·7	59·3	84·0
1,022	1,175	1·9	10·5	13·0	17·0	24·6
723	782	1·4	13·5	19·2	25·6	39·5
705	924	1·2	3·0	3·2	3·6	5·0
6,495	9,507	21·9	80·8	115·1	154·0	233·1
4,817	**8,392**	**5·3**	**59·0**	**85·7**	**112·3**	**208·9**
1,444	2,243	2·0	9·8	17·6	27·9	53·6
2,801	5,206	2·3	31·5	44·4	56·0	112·7
572	943	1·0	17·7	23·7	28·3	42·7
3,328	**2,665**	**2·0**	**28·5**	**36·3**	**49·6**	**60·7**
1,366	1,631	1·2	17·6	20·9	29·5	42·3
1,962	1,034	0·7	11·0	15·4	20·1	18·5
9,604	**39,675**	**71·2**	**324·1**	**433·1**	**563·2**	**847·1**

Here and in the following tables central government = federal government
he U.S., and local government = state and local government in the U.S.

amount retained by companies. One item, however, income from productive activity abroad, no longer appears as a separate entry: it is included in items 1c (i) and (ii), following the *Blue Book*, which does not specify how it is distributed among the various domestic sectors but only gives the total figure for it. On the other hand, as a result of separating the private from the public sector, a new item, benefits and grants received from public authorities, makes its appearance under the heading of *income from transfers*. Various relatively small transfers make their appearance in item 2c, which is composed of grants from companies to non-profit institutions *less* net gifts and direct taxes paid to the rest of the world.

The outgoings of the account are also subdivided and expanded. Private consumers' expenditure is broken up into a number of commodity groups and saving is divided between persons and companies. Here too a new item appears, *taxes on income*, again as a consequence of separating the sectors.

As to the sources of the figures, for Britain they are to be found as follows. Item 1a corresponds to income from employment in table 2 of the *Blue Book*; item 1b is equal to income from self-employment in table 2 *less* the personal sector's depreciation on assets other than dwellings in table 58 and *less* the personal sector's stock appreciation in table 67; item 1c (i) is equal to rent, dividends and net interest in table 2 *less* the sector's depreciation on dwellings in table 58; and item 1c (ii) is simply the undistributed income of companies as we have defined it in Chapter I. Items 2a and 2b correspond to total grants to persons in tables 37 and 41 respectively; and item 2c is equal to current transfers to charities from companies in table 2 *less* transfers abroad (net) and taxes paid abroad in the same table. The subdivisions of consumers' expenditure in items 3a to 3h come mainly from table 22 and can easily be traced there; the only conceptual difference is that we have reverted, on the basis of unpublished information, to the old *Blue Book* practice of including food bought in restaurants, cafés and the like in category 3a, food, rather than in catering which is part of category 3h. Item 4a corresponds to national insurance etc. contributions in table 2; item 4b corresponds to payments of British taxes on income in table 2; and item 4c corresponds to payments of British taxes on other income in table 26. Item 5a is equal to saving *plus* additions to tax reserves, both in table 2, *less* the personal sector's total depreciation and stock appreciation in tables 58 and 67; and item 5b is equal to item 1c (ii) *less* item 4c.

For America, item 1a is the same as 1.10.2 in [84] and in the *Survey*, this and other references being most easily traced in [84] where the rows of the tables are numbered; item 1b is the same as 1.10.12; item 1c (i) is equal to the sum of 2.1.12, 2.1.13 and 2.1.14 *less* 2.1.25; and item 1c (ii) is equal to 1.10.18 *less* 1.10.22. Item 2a is the same as 3.1.26; item 2b is the same as 3.3.30; and item 2c is equal to 1.9.15 *less* 2.1.26. Item 3 is the same as 1.1.2, and its components can be found in table 2.5: thus the sum of 3a and 3b is equal to the sum of 2.5.2 through 2.5.5, and its allocation between food and drink is given in a note to the table; items 3c, 3d and 3e are equal to 2.5.6, 2.5.7 and 2.5.21 respectively; item 3f (i) is equal to the sum of 2.5.27, 2.5.28 and 2.5.82; item 3f (ii) is equal to the sum of 2.5.62 and 2.5.81; item 3g is equal to the sum of 2.5.68 and 2.5.72; and item 3h is the sum of all the components of consumers' expenditure not enumerated above. The categories we have used do not follow exactly the American classification of private consumers' expenditure but are roughly matched, in the interests of comparability, with those in the *Blue Book*; hence, for instance, the considerable difference between our figures for major durables and the American ones for all durables, which in 1969 amounted to \$90·0 milliard as opposed to the \$64·1 milliard given by us.

To return to our list of sources. Item 4a is the same as 1.9.10; item 4b is equal to 2.1.21 *less* the sum of 3.1.5 and 3.3.4, which are treated by us as paid out of capital rather than income account; and item 4c is the same as 1.10.20. Item 5a is equal to the sum of 2.1.27, 3.1.5 and 3.3.4, and to these might be added 1.9.11 which, however, is zero in all the years shown in our tables; and finally, item 5b is equal to the sum of 1.10.23 and 1.10.24.

If table 7 is compared with table 1 above, it will be noticed that total incomings in table 7 are the same as private income in table 1; and that interest (net), profits and rent retained by companies in table 7 are the same as undistributed income of companies before tax in table 1. In other words, table 7 is, on the income side, an elaboration of the first three entries of table 1, and in addition gives details about the corresponding outlays. The comparison also illustrates the fact that with a coherent set of tables, such as the *Blue Book* and the *Survey* provide, a given total can be reached by more than one route.

Let us now pass on to the public sector. The income and outlay of this sector are set out in table 8 below.

The arrangement of this table is similar to that of table 7. In setting out income from productive activity, interest paid is deducted from interest received, that is the interest on government debt is treated as negative income to the government. It appears, of course, as a positive income to the recipients, whether public or private, and so cancels out in the national income except for that part of it which goes abroad, whose positive counterpart is in the rest of the world.

Income from transfers consists mainly of indirect taxes (net) and taxes on income. The former are exactly as in table 3 above. The latter are subdivided to show the net receipts of the three sub-sectors of the public sector. Public corporations have negative receipts since they pay but do not receive taxes on income.

These two categories of taxes are by far the most important but they do not make up quite the whole of the government's revenue from taxation. The missing element is *taxes on capital*, mainly death duties, which together with taxes on income make up *direct taxes*. These capital taxes are treated by us as capital transfers and so disappear in the consolidated account for capital transactions (table 4 above). The consequence of this treatment is that private saving is reckoned before paying these taxes and public saving is reckoned before receiving them.

The outlay side of table 8 shows the outgoings of the public sector divided between expenditure on goods and services, current transfers to the personal sector and saving.

For Britain, the sources of the figures in table 8 are as follows. Item 1a is equal to total allocation of income in table 33 of the *Blue Book* *less* all payments of interest and dividends in the same table and *less* the depreciation and stock appreciation of public corporations in tables 58 and 67; item 1b is equal to gross trading surplus *plus* rent, dividends and interest *less* debt interest, all in table 4, *less* the relevant depreciation in table 58 and, in principle, *less* the relevant stock appreciation in table 67, though in practice this figure has been zero since 1955; item 1c is equal to gross trading surplus *plus* rent, dividends and interest *less* debt interest, all in table 5, *less* the relevant depreciation in table 58. Item 2a (i) is the excess of taxes on expenditure over subsidies, both in table 4, and item 2a (ii) is the excess of rates over housing subsidies in table 5. Item 2b (i) is the negative of payments of British taxes on income in table 33; item 2b (ii) is the sum of taxes on income and national insurance etc. contributions in table 4; and item 2b (iii) is blank because in Britain local authorities do not levy taxes on income. Item 2c is equal to the excess of current grants from overseas governments over current grants paid abroad in table 4. Items 3a (i) and (ii) correspond respectively to military defence and to the national health service in table 37, and item 3a (iii) is obtained from the same table by subtracting these two items from total expenditure on goods and services; item 3b (i) corresponds to education in table 41 and item 3b (ii) is equal to all other expenditure on goods and services in the same table. Item 4a corresponds to national insurance benefits and other current grants to the personal sector in table 4, and item 4b corresponds to current grants to the personal sector in table 5. Item 5a is equal to the sum of items 1a and 2b (i); item 5b is equal to the current surplus in table 4 *less* depreciation and stock appreciation in tables 58

TABL

Income and Outla

	United Kingdom £ *million*			
	1938	1954	1959	196
1. Income from productive activity†	**–183**	**–578**	**–695**	**–55**
(*a*) Public corporations	–4	–57	–195	–4
(*b*) Central government	–194	–453	–421	–40
(*c*) Local government	15	–68	–79	–11
2. Income from transfers				
(*a*) Indirect taxes (net)	**585**	**2,082**	**2,831**	**3,94**
(i) central government	378	1,642	2,145	2,89
(ii) local government	207	440	686	1,05
(*b*) Taxes on income	**493**	**2,642**	**3,644**	**4,96**
(i) public corporations	0	–37	–11	–
(ii) central government	493	2,679	3,655	4,97
(iii) local government	—	—	—	—
(*c*) Current grants from abroad (net)	**–8**	**–20**	**–82**	**–16**
Total incomings	**887**	**4,126**	**5,698**	**8,19**
3. Consumers' expenditure	**772**	**3,185**	**4,001**	**5,51**
(*a*) Central government	454			
(i) military defence	..	1,520	1,512	1,92
(ii) health service	..	470	683	94
(iii) other	..	373	538	69
(*b*) Local government	318			
(i) education	..	358	602	93
(ii) other	..	464	666	1,01
4. Benefits and grants to persons ..	**275**	**944**	**1,555**	**2,25**
(*a*) Central government	250	924	1,518	2,18
(*b*) Local government	25	20	37	7
5. Saving†	**–160**	**–3**	**142**	**42**
(*a*) Public corporations	–4	–94	–206	–4
(*b*) Central government	–177	120	335	39
(*c*) Local government	21	–29	13	7
Total outgoings	**887**	**4,126**	**5,698**	**8,19**

* Components do not always add up to totals because of rounding-off erro
† Does not include residual error or statistical discrepancy.

8
of the Public Sector

	United States* $ *milliard (billion)*				
1969	1938	1954	1959	1964	1969
–745	**–0·8**	**–4·0**	**–5·1**	**–6·1**	**–9·7**
–208	—	—	—	—	—
–315	–0·6	–5·0	–6·4	–8·3	–13·1
–222	–0·2	1·0	1·3	2·2	3·4
7,024	**8·6**	**28·3**	**39·3**	**54·2**	**80·6**
5,452	1·6	8·6	10·4	11·9	14·5
1,572	6·9	19·7	28·9	42·3	66·1
8,564	**5·3**	**59·0**	**85·7**	**112·3**	**208·9**
–15	—	—	—	—	—
8,579	3·9	53·1	75·8	96·3	177·9
—	1·5	5·9	9·9	16·0	31·0
–175	**0·0**	**0·0**	**0·0**	**0·0**	**0·0**
14,668	**13·1**	**83·3**	**119·9**	**160·4**	**279·8**
8,118	**10·7**	**63·3**	**80·9**	**108·2**	**184·2**
	4·8				
2,267	..	38·6	43·8	48·6	77·3
1,489 1,124 }	..	5·5	6·3	12·9	20·9
	5·9				
1,553	..	8·4	14·4	22·6	41·6
1,685	..	10·8	16·4	24·1	44·4
3,930	**2·4**	**14·9**	**24·9**	**34·2**	**61·6**
3,783	1·2	11·5	20·1	27·8	50·0
147	1·2	3·4	4·8	6·5	11·5
2,620	**0·0**	**5·1**	**14·1**	**18·0**	**34·0**
–223	—	—	—	—	—
2,779	–1·9	–1·8	2·7	0·2	10·9
64	1·9	6·9	11·4	17·8	23·1
14,668	**13·1**	**83·3**	**119·9**	**160·4**	**279·8**

and 67; and item 5c is equal to the current surplus in table 5 *less* depreciation in table 58.

As to the American sources, items 1a, 2b (i) and 5a are left blank because public corporations do not appear in the *Survey* as a separate category but are treated as part of central and local government. Item 1b is the negative of 3.1.29, and item 1c is equal to 3.3.32 *less* 3.3.31. Item 2a (i) is equal to 3.1.9 *less* 3.1.30; item 2a (ii) is the same as 3.3.10; item 2b (ii) is equal to the sum of 3.1.2, 3.1.8 and 3.1.18 *less* 3.1.5; item 2b (iii) is equal to the sum of 3.3.2, 3.3.9 and 3.3.22 *less* 3.3.4; and item 2c is zero in every year because net government transfers to foreigners are treated by us as capital transfers. Item 3 is equal to 1.1.20 *less* the sum of 3.1.22 and 3.3.27; and the details are taken from table 3.11 (for instance, 3a (i) is equal to 3.11.2 *less* 3.11.4). Item 4a is the same as 3.1.26, and item 4b is the same as 3.3.30. Item 5b is equal to the sum of 3.1.22, 3.1.27 and 3.1.31 *less* 3.1.5; and item 5c is equal to the sum of 3.3.27 and 3.3.33 *less* 3.3.4.

If we consolidate tables 7 and 8, adding together the corresponding entries in the two tables and cancelling out the items which appear as incomings in one account and as outgoings in the other, we obtain a new table which is similar to table 3 above but more detailed. In making a comparison we must remember that in table 3 the residual error is included in national income from domestic production and also in saving, whereas it is not included anywhere in tables 7 and 8. Thus from the outgoings side of tables 7 and 8 we obtain for Britain in 1969: a total for consumers' expenditure of £28,618 + 8,118 = 36,736 million; and a total for saving, including the residual error, of £2,665 + 2,620 − 342 = 4,943 million. These are the two main totals on the outgoings side of table 3, but when we come to the incomings side the position is a little more complicated because of the way we have chosen to arrange the detailed entries in tables 7 and 8. Thus if we combine the entries for income from productive activity and add in the residual error we obtain £35,809 − 745 − 342 = 34,722 million.

This is not equal to the national income of £34,907 million shown in table 3 but the missing bits can easily be found, as we shall see in a moment.

To continue with the consolidation, indirect taxes (net), item 2a of table 8, do not cancel out and so their total, £7,024 million, remains in the consolidated table. When we consolidate taxes on income, we are left with a figure of £8,564 − 8,392 = 172 million on the incomings side of the account, and this represents British taxes on income paid by foreigners. The only remaining incomings which do not cancel out are item 2c in each of the tables: item 2c in table 7 is made up of current transfers to charities from companies, £35 million, *less* personal payments of foreign taxes on income, − £22 million, and *less* current transfers abroad (net) from the personal sector, − £77 million; and item 2c in table 8 is simply the negative of current transfers abroad made by the central government, − £175 million.

The last two figures in this list, with their signs changed, sum to £252 million. This is the missing item of current transfers abroad (net) shown among the outgoings of table 3.

The remaining items, £172 + 35 − 22 = 185 million, are the missing bits of the national income: £34,722 + 185 = 34,907 million. It is not difficult to explain these additions. In the first place, it will be remembered from section 1 of Chapter I that in the *Blue Book* international transfers of direct taxes are treated as part of international payments of property income. In the second place, we decided to define the retained income of companies to exclude grants to charities and foreign taxes on income, with the consequence that company saving is simply undistributed income *less* British taxes on income.

Tables 7 and 8 illustrate the obvious fact that income is constantly being modified by a complicated series of transfers, so that the income concept which is relevant to the spending and saving behaviour of the economic units that make up sectors is not at the same stage of the redistributive process for each sector. The time has now come to face these difficulties and this we shall do in the two sections that follow.

2. *Income Originating and Income Retained*

In the *Blue Book* the two main sectors distinguished in the preceding section are further subdivided: the private sector into persons and companies; and the public sector into public corporations, central government and local authorities. All the income from productive activity, or *factor income*, arising in Britain is generated, to a greater or lesser extent, in these five sectors. Table 13 of the *Blue Book* shows how much income originates in each sector. The *factor income originating* in each sector can be divided into two parts: income from employment, which includes wages, salaries and all employers' contributions; and other income, which includes income from self-employment, profits, net interest and rent, from which we must deduct, as usual, depreciation and stock appreciation in table 58. The sum of all the incomes originating in the five sectors, net of depreciation and stock appreciation, is quite simply the domestic income.

Much of the income which originates in a sector is not retained by it but is paid out to and retained by other sectors. Thus all the income from employment which originates in the company sector and in the three public sectors is paid out to and retained by the personal sector. In a similar way, companies pay dividends to shareholders, individuals pay interest to banks, building societies, hire-purchase companies and so on, the government pays interest to the holders of the public debt, and all domestic sectors pay out to and receive from the rest of the world some property income. The *factor income retained* in each sector can be measured by adding to the income originating in that sector all factor income received from the other sectors and from the rest of the world and subtracting all factor income paid out by the sector. In principle, the sum of all the factor incomes retained by the domestic sectors is the national income.

In practice, however, since the *Blue Book* defines international payments of property income to include international transfers of direct taxes, in order to agree with the official figures it is desirable to have three classifications of factor income: income originating, income retained, and income retained after adjustment for international direct-tax transfers. These three classifications and the connections between them are set out in table 9 below.

The first three columns of table 9 show how much factor income originated in 1969 in each of the domestic sectors and how much in the rest of the world. For instance, we can see from column 1 that of the £27,174 million of income from employment, £2,489 million, or about 9 per cent, originated in the personal sector and the remainder, adding up to £24,685 million, originated in the other domestic sectors. Column 2 shows where the other income originated. And the grand total in column 3 is the sum of the domestic income, £34,456 million, as in table 1 above, *plus* the factor income arising from British productive activity abroad, £2,092 million, as given in table 7 of the *Blue Book*: £34,456 + 2,092 = 36,548 million. As we shall see, this total remains unchanged throughout this table and the next.

Columns 4 through 6 show the redistribution of income from employment, all of which flowed into the personal sector. Columns 7 through 9 show the redistribution of other factor income. Here the flows go both ways. For instance, the personal sector received £4,023 million and paid out £963 million. The second of these figures is given in the fifth line of table 24 of the *Blue Book*; the first can be deduced as follows. We have seen in table 7 that other income from productive activity received by the personal sector in 1969 amounted in all to £2,547 + 4,111 = 6,658 million. But the second figure is net of interest paid, and so to get the gross receipts of the sector we must add back the interest paid: £6,658 + 963 = 7,621 million. Of this we see from table 9 that £3,598 million originated in the personal sector itself. Thus £7,621 − 3,598

TABL
Redistributio
From Income Originating (Domestic Incon
United Kingdo

	Factor income originating		
	Income from employment	Other income	Tota
	(1)	(2)	(3)
Persons	2,489	3,598	6,08
Companies	16,860	3,048	19,90
Public corporations	2,721	416	3,13
Central government	2,503	–3	2,50
Local authorities	2,601	565	3,16
Residual error	...	...	–34
All domestic sectors	...	...	34,45
The rest of the world	0	2,092	2,09
Grand total	...	...	36,54

	Factor income retained		
	Income from employment	Other income	Tota
	(10)	(11)	(12)
Persons	27,174	6,658	33,83
Companies	0	2,790	2,79
Public corporation ...	0	–208	–20
Central government ...	0	–315	–31
Local authorities ...	0	–222	–22
Residual error ...	...	...	–34
All domestic sectors	...	...	35,53
The rest of the world ...	0	1,013	1,01
Grand total	...	...	36,54

ıong Sectors:
Income Retained (National Income)
69 (£ *million*)

Redistribution: receipts and payments of factor income					
Income from employment			Other income		
Incomings (4)	*less* Outgoings (5)	Net gain or loss (–) (6)	Incomings (7)	*less* Outgoings (8)	Net gain or loss (–) (9)
24,685	–0	24,685	4,023	–963	3,060
0	–16,860	–16,860	3,617	–3,875	–258
0	–2,721	–2,721	89	–713	–624
0	–2,503	–2,503	975	1,287	–312
0	–2,601	–2,601	105	–892	–787
24,685	–24,685	0	8,809	–7,730	1,079
0	–0	0	1,013	–2,092	–1,079
24,685	–24,685	0	9,822	–9,822	0

Redistribution: direct taxes to and from abroad			Adjusted factor income retained
Incomings (13)	*less* Outgoings (14)	Net gain or loss (–) (15)	(16)
0	–22	–22	33,810
0	–778	–788	2,012
0	–0	0	–208
172	–0	172	–143
0	–0	0	–222
			–342
172	–800	–628	34,907
800	–172	628	1,641
972	–972	0	36,548

= 4,023 million must have originated somewhere else. By somewhat similar means the other figures in columns 7 through 9 can all be derived from the *Blue Book*.

Columns 10 through 12 show the results of this first round of redistributions. The figures in column 10 are obtained by summing the corresponding sector figures in columns 1 and 6; and those in column 11, by summing the corresponding figures in columns 2 and 9. Thus all the income from employment, £2,489 + 24,685 = 27,174 million, was retained by the personal sector and so was the greatest part of other factor income, £3,598 + 3,060 = 6,658 million, the remainder being shared between the company sector, which retained £3,048 − 258 = 2,790 million, and the rest of the world, which retained £2,092 − 1,079 = 1,013 million. The three public sectors were losers. The grand total in column 12 is now the sum of all factor incomes arising from British productive activity at home and abroad, £35,535 million, *plus* the factor income arising from foreign productive activity in Britain, £1,013 million.

As we said above, the former of these two figures should, in principle, equal the national income; however, because of the *Blue Book* treatment of international transfers of direct taxes, it does not. Accordingly, columns 13 through 15 show the incoming and outgoing transfers and their balances; and column 16 shows retained factor income after adjustment for these transfers. The total for the domestic sectors, £34,907 million, is now equal to the national income as defined in the *Blue Book* and shown in table 1 above. And the national income *plus* the property income and direct taxes paid by Britain to the rest of the world equal the same grand total as before: £34,907 + 1,641 = 36,548 million.

3. *The Contribution and Use of Resources*

Let us now consider the chain of redistributions linking the factor income retained by the sectors, which measures their contribution to the production of goods and services, with their net final expenditure, which measures their use of these same goods and services. This chain of redistributions is shown in table 10.

Table 10 starts off with income retained after adjustment for international direct-tax transfers, as given in the final column of table 9, and sets out four further rounds of redistributions.

The first round, shown in columns 2 through 4, consists mainly of cash transfers from the central government to the personal sector and to local authorities. The incoming flow of £4,141 million into the personal sector is made up of: grants from companies, £35 million; benefits and grants from the central government, £3,783 million; benefits and grants from local authorities, £147 million; and gifts from the rest of the world, £176 million. The outgoing flow consists entirely of gifts to the rest of the world, £253 million. The net gain to the personal sector is £3,888 million. A notable feature of this round of redistributions is the large transfer of £2,099 million received by local authorities from the central government; in 1959 the corresponding figure was £711 million, or about one third.

The results of this round are shown in column 5. The net gainers are persons, local authorities and the rest of the world. It will be noticed that if the figures for persons and companies are added together, we obtain a total of *private income before tax*, £37,698 + 1,977 = 39,675 million, which is the same as the total of table 7 above.

The second round, shown in columns 6 through 8, consists entirely of taxes on income paid by persons, companies and public corporations to the central government. The total gain to the government is £8,407 million. If we subtract from this figure the £15 million paid by public corporations and add the £172 million of direct taxes paid by the rest of the world (column 14 of table 9 above), we obtain the net revenue accruing to the public sector as a whole from taxes on income: £8,407 − 15 + 172 = 8,564 million, as in table 8 above.

TAB
Redistributio
From Income Retained (National Income) to Use
United Kingdo

	Adjusted factor income retained	Redistribution: grants, benefits, gifts etc.		
		Incomings	*less* Outgoings	Net ga or loss
	(1)	(2)	(3)	(4)
Persons	33,810	4,141	–253	3,888
Companies	2,012	0	–35	–35
Public corporations ..	–208	0	–0	0
Central government ..	–143	0	–6,057	–6,057
Local authorities ..	–222	2,099	–147	1,952
Residual error ..	–342			
All domestic sectors ..	34,907	6,240	–6,492	–252
The rest of the world	1,641	428	–176	252
Grand total	36,548	6,668	–6,668	0

	Disposable income*	Redistribution: indirect taxes (net)		
		Incomings	*less* Outgoings	Net gai or loss
	(9)	(10)	(11)	(12)
Persons	30,249	0	–5,688	–5,688
Companies	1,034	0	–153	–153
Public corporations ..	–223	0	–27	–27
Central government ..	2,207	5,452	–415	5,037
Local authorities ..	1,730	1,572	–358	1,214
Residual error ..	–342			
All domestic sectors ..	34,655	7,024	–6,641	383
The rest of the world	1,893	0	–383	–383
Grand total	36,548	7,024	–7,024	0

* This term is appropriate to the personal sector only.

ong Sectors:
sources (Consumption and Net Investment)
9 (£ *million*)

Income before tax*	Redistribution: internal taxes on income		
	Incomings	*less* Outgoings	Net gain or loss (–)
(5)	(6)	(7)	(8)
37,698	0	–7,449	–7,449
1,977	0	–943	–943
–208	0	–15	–15
–6,200	8,407	–0	8,407
1,730	0	–0	0
–342			
34,655	8,407	–8,407	0
1,893	0	–0	0
36,548	8,407	–8,407	0

Final income	Redistribution: net borrowing and net capital transfers received	Use of resources
(13)	(14)	(15)
24,561	–1,198	23,363
881	977	1,858
–250	579	329
7,244	–2,387	4,857
2,944	1,271	4,215
–342	342	
35,038	–416	34,622
1,510	416	1,926
36,548	0	36,548

The results of this round of redistributions are shown in column 9. For the personal sector, the income total after this round is usually termed *disposable income* and is available for spending or saving. For the corporate sectors it represents simply corporate saving, private or public, since there is no final consumption by these sectors. These corporate savings, £1,034 million and –£233 million respectively, can be traced in tables 7 and 8.

The third round, shown in columns 10 through 12, relates to the purchase taxes, excise duties etc. (net of subsidies) payable in respect of the final expenditures of the sectors. In section 3 of Chapter II indirect taxes, which are taxes on sales, were treated as a cost of production because they are collected from the producer, but since this cost is ultimately passed on by the producer to the purchaser, they are shown in table 10 as paid by the purchasing sectors. The estimates are based on table 46 of the *Blue Book*, with some necessary elaborations. Thus the £592 million of taxes attributed to public authorities' expenditure on goods and services have been divided between central and local government in proportion to their expenditures as given in tables 37 and 41 respectively. The total of £656 million attributed to gross domestic capital formation has been allocated among the five domestic sectors and the rest of the world as follows: first, this total has been divided *pro rata* between the amount attributable to depreciation and that attributable to net domestic capital formation; second, the amount attributable to depreciation has been allocated *pro rata* between personal consumption, central and local government consumption, and exports; third, the amount attributable to net domestic capital formation has been allocated *pro rata* among the net investment of the sectors. Finally, the amounts payable in respect of net investment have been added, sector by sector, to the amounts payable in respect of consumption. Thus we can see from column 11 that the personal sector is estimated to have paid £5,688 million of indirect taxes (net), the company sector £153 million, and so on. The net gainers at this stage are of course the public sectors, which receive in all £7,024 million, as shown in table 8 above, and pay out (to each other) £27 + 415 + 358 = 800 million.

The totals reached after this round of redistributions are shown in column 13 and represent the sectors' *final income*. If the sectors spent all their final income on the purchase of final product, the amounts of indirect taxes they would pay or receive would be slightly different and the totals in column 13 (which would consequently be different too) would represent the sectors' 'command over resources', that is to say the amount of goods and services valued at factor cost which each sector could buy.

Sectors, however, do not use the whole of their final income to buy goods and services but decrease (or increase) their purchasing power by lending or borrowing, making or receiving capital gifts. The fourth round of redistributions relates to these flows of capital finance. In this case the *Blue Book* enables us to derive only net figures: net borrowing and net capital transfers received. These net flows are shown in column 14. As can be seen, the two sectors which, on balance, give up some of their purchasing power are the personal sector and the central government. The sectors whose purchasing power is increased are the two corporate sectors, local authorities and the rest of the world.

The totals resulting from this round of redistributions are shown in column 15. They represent the sectors' *use of resources*, that is to say their actual purchases of final product, valued at factor cost, for the purpose of consumption or net additions to their stock of capital goods.

If we compare the entries in this last column with those relating to factor income retained in column 12 of table 9, we can see how far individual sectors put more into the pot of production than they withdraw from it, and *vice versa*. Not surprisingly, persons and companies are net contributors while all the public sectors and the rest of the world are net users. For the personal sector, for instance, retained factor income in

1969 was £33,832 million. Non-tax transfers *less* payments of international direct taxes amounted to £3,866 million, giving a figure of £37,698 million for income before tax, which is the income concept used in table 7 above and, indeed, in table 1. Internal direct taxes amounted to £7,449 million, leaving a figure of £30,249 million for disposable income. Indirect taxes (net) amounted to £5,688 million, leaving a figure of £24,561 million for final income. Finally, net lending and net capital transfers to other sectors amounted to £1,198 million, leaving a figure of £23,363 million for use of resources. If we put the retained factor income of the personal sector equal to 100, we can see that personal income before tax was 111, disposable income was 90, final income was 73 and use of resources was 69.

One last point. It will be noticed that throughout table 10, although at each round of redistributions the composition of the grand total changes, its amount is always the same. This brings out clearly the fundamental difference between income from productive activity and income from transfers mentioned in section 1 of Chapter I: only productive activity can generate income; transfers may enrich one sector at the expense of another but they do not add one penny to the total of income available.

So much for redistributions between sectors. Let us now see how far we can measure the differential effects of the various stages of redistribution on the components of a sector, specifically on households of different size and composition and in different income ranges.

4. *Redistributions over Households*

The *Blue Book* does not subdivide any further the sectors distinguished in the preceding section and so it cannot be used to examine the question just raised. For this purpose we must turn to the studies of the incidence of taxes and social service benefits which appear from time to time in *Economic Trends* [60] and, in particular, to that contained in the issue for

February 1971, which provides information for 1969. This study is based on the *Family Expenditure Survey Report for 1969* [72] and on similar reports for earlier years.

The calculations for 1969 are based on a sample of just over seven thousand households classified by size, composition, income range and other characteristics. The initial income concept is termed *original income* and is defined as 'the sum of the incomes in cash and kind (as measured in the survey) of all members of the household before the deduction of taxes and before the addition of the State benefits included in this analysis'. The taxes and other transfers included are restricted to those paid to and received from the central government and local authorities, but these are, of course, by far the most important. Their precise composition is set out in [60].

Before 1969 the concept of original income was roughly comparable to the concept of retained factor income as defined in section 2 above. In 1969, however, a substantial change was made; it was decided that employers' contributions to national insurance and national health services should, in contrast with earlier practice and with the conventions used in the national accounts, be excluded from original income. The effect of this new definition is to reduce the average original income of all households in the sample from £1,572 to £1,519. The adjustment to the old definition is given in [60] for the average household and for households classified by size and composition, but not for households classified by size, composition and income range. Thus, while we can indicate the effects of redistribution on the average household in a manner comparable with the results of the preceding section, we must adopt the new definition in setting out the detailed figures for different types of household.

The span of redistribution covered in [60] goes from original income, through income before tax and disposable income, to income after all taxes and benefits, which is roughly comparable to final income in the preceding section. Working on the pre-1969 definition and omitting benefits in kind, we obtain the following series for the average household in the sample: original income, £1,572; income before tax, £1,732; disposable income, £1,421; income after all taxes and benefits, £1,116. If original income is put at 100, the series runs: 100, 110, 90 and 71. This progression is very similar to that derived from tables 9 and 10 for the personal sector as a whole.

Let us now turn to the detailed estimates given in [60]. A small part of these is set out in table 11 below. Here the figures include direct benefits in kind and are based on the new definition, that is to say they exclude from original income employers' contributions to national insurance and national health services. The data are grouped by selected ranges of original income and, within each income range, by household size and composition. The first column of the table shows the number of households of each type on which the estimates are based. For instance, there are in the sample 606 households consisting of one adult with an original income of less than £260 a year (as many as 528 of these being households of retired people, which in [60] are tabulated separately). As can be seen, the numbers for different types of household vary enormously; information is given only for types of which the sample number is ten or more.

If we consider first the average results for the different income ranges we can see, by comparing the figures in columns 4 and 14, that in the lowest range as much as 85 per cent of income after all taxes and benefits (final income) arises in the course of the process of redistribution: $(465 - 69)/465 = 0{\cdot}85$ approximately. In the second range shown in table 11 the percentage falls to 37 per cent and in the third range it falls to 6 per cent. Beyond this point, original income exceeds income after all taxes and benefits and, on average, households make a net contribution, giving more than they gain in the redistributive process. The use of averages in this way, though it makes the general point that poor households gain and rich ones lose through redistribution, obscures the fact that the size and composition of the average household change as we go up the income scale. We can avoid this distortion by comparing the contribution of a given type of household in different income ranges. For instance, the net contribution of a household composed of two adults in the fifth and highest income range is £2,315 – 1,555 = 760; of the same type of household in the fourth income range, £1,313 – 949 = 364; in the third income range, £750 – 760 = –10; in the second, £418 – 717 = –299; and in the first and lowest, £82 – 541 = –459.

But the redistributive process operates not only to help poor families at the expense of rich ones but also to help large families, in particular families with many children, at the expense of small ones. For instance, if we concentrate on the fourth income range and look at households with two adults and nought up to four children, we find that the net contributions are £364, £282, £155, –£12 and –£133. Thus, while the households in this income range make, on average, a net contribution, those with three or four children are net beneficiaries. If we take the highest income range, we find that all the corresponding household types make a net contribution, the figures being £760, £613, £550, £322 and £68.

This information throws a great deal of light on the redistributive activities of the state. Substantially similar information is available in [60] for odd years from 1957 to 1961 and thereafter for every year, so that changes in the incidence of taxes and social service benefits can be traced over a span of years. It must be recognized, however, that the estimates are subject to sampling errors, so that some of the less numerous groups of households may not be represented quite fairly. For instance, in the case of households consisting of two adults and one child in our third income range, the income after all taxes and benefits, £705, looks somewhat low and out of line, particularly in relation to the comparatively high figure of original income, £771. But sampling errors are something we must all learn to live with, partly because there is need for a wide variety of information that can best be collected by

TABL

The Effect of Government Taxes a
United Kingdo
(

Number of households in the sample	Range of original income	Household size and composition*	Original income	Direct benefits in cash	Direct benefits in kind	Income before tax
(1)	(2)	(3)	(4)	(5)	(6)	(7)
606	Up to £259	1a	63	315	60	438
368		2a	82	483	106	670
11		2a 2c	76	439	336	850
18		3a	100	640	152	902
1,069	**All households in the range**		**69**	**397**	**99**	**565**
43	£382–459	1a	421	178	40	637
51		2a	418	387	131	936
111	**All households in the range**		**419**	**310**	**142**	**871**
56	£676–815	1a	737	57	41	835
97		2a	750	226	100	1,076
27		2a 1c	771	92	186	1,048
16		2a 2c	753	160	193	1,106
13		2a 3c	767	193	268	1,227
16		3a	746	420	208	1,374
257	**All households in the range**		**749**	**191**	**155**	**1,093**
47	£1,196–1,447	1a	1,310	68	38	1,416
226		2a	1,313	84	64	1,461
141		2a 1c	1,324	34	156	1,514
155		2a 2c	1,329	72	234	1,635
53		2a 3c	1,332	153	344	1,827
26		2a 4c	1,308	177	486	1,971
66		3a	1,312	231	218	1,761
17		3a 1c	1,312	170	357	1,838
12		3a 2c	1,358	219	297	1,875
10		4a	1,294	398	170	1,862
788	**All households in the range**		**1,319**	**110**	**191**	**1,621**
12	£2,122–2,565	1a	2,345	31	29	2,404
160		2a	2,315	43	57	2,414
75		2a 1c	2,315	16	182	2,511
99		2a 2c	2,323	56	228	2,607
51		2a 3c	2,328	106	361	2,795
13		2a 4c	2,290	170	505	2,964
119		3a	2,312	85	156	2,553
42		3a 1c	2,338	49	278	2,663
29		3a 2c	2,338	110	460	2,908
30		4a	2,339	195	206	2,931
701	**All households in the range**		**2,323**	**80**	**222**	**2,625**
7,008	All households in the sample		**1,519**	**160**	**179**	**1,858**

* The symbol a denotes adult (person 16 and over) and the symbol c denotes child (person under
Note: Components do not always add up to totals because of rounding-off errors.

ansfers on Different Types of Household.
59
ear)

s Employees' contributions to national insurance (8)	*less* Income tax and surtax (9)	Income after direct taxes and benefits (10)	Housing subsidies (11)	*less* Indirect taxes paid directly (12)	*less* Indirect taxes paid indirectly (13)	Income after all taxes and benefits (14)
0	−2	436	16	−56	−26	369
0	0	670	17	−102	−44	541
−11	26	865	3	−155	−66	646
−10	−14	878	12	−126	−66	697
−1	**−1**	**563**	**16**	**− 79**	**−35**	**465**
−6	−38	593	10	−99	−37	467
−7	−29	900	11	−136	−57	717
−8	**−26**	**837**	**13**	**−131**	**−52**	**666**
−33	−79	723	7	−118	−45	567
−30	−68	978	11	−164	−67	760
−53	−25	970	17	−205	−77	705
−43	59	1,122	13	−176	−66	894
−38	9	1,198	21	−223	−93	903
−40	−42	1,292	27	−203	−75	1,042
−34	**−46**	**1,013**	**15**	**−167**	**−67**	**795**
−43	−241	1,132	4	−199	−66	871
−57	−165	1,239	14	−223	−82	949
−60	−118	1,336	12	−222	−84	1,042
−59	−112	1,464	13	−216	−87	1,174
−58	−106	1,663	22	−246	−95	1,344
−62	−81	1,828	6	−287	−106	1,441
−64	−131	1,566	19	−271	−96	1,219
−68	−80	1,690	16	−258	−104	1,344
−72	−78	1,725	19	−254	−104	1,368
−82	−140	1,640	28	−356	−133	1,180
−59	**−134**	**1,428**	**15**	**−232**	**−88**	**1,123**
−42	−492	1,870	1	−192	−83	1,594
−78	−361	1,975	4	−318	−106	1,555
−73	−327	2,111	3	−297	−115	1,702
−65	−344	2,198	9	−314	−120	1,773
−64	−297	2,434	6	−301	−133	2,006
−65	−217	2,682	4	−331	−134	2,222
−95	−317	2,141	15	−373	−126	1,657
−93	−259	2,311	16	−380	−146	1,801
−84	−247	2,577	5	−351	−148	2,083
−113	−289	2,334	13	−412	−132	1,802
−83	**−311**	**2,231**	**10**	**−342**	**−125**	**1,775**
−54	**−204**	**1,600**	**13**	**−249**	**−94**	**1,271**

sampling methods and partly because sample surveys are expensive and their coverage cannot be expanded indefinitely. With a survey that is well designed and carried out they can do very little harm, provided the reader is aware of their existence and makes allowance for them in interpreting the figures he reads.

CHAPTER IV

COMPARISONS OVER TIME

1. *Product Totals at Constant Prices*

IF WE look at item 6 of table 1 above we see that in 1969 the gross domestic product of Britain was £45,174 million. From the *Blue Book* we can find out that in 1963 it was £30,245 million, that is to say it had increased *in value* in six years by 49 per cent. But without more information this comparison is not very enlightening, since we do not know how far the rise was due to more products and how far it was due to higher prices. Accordingly we must now try to find out by how much the gross domestic product changed *in quantity* over the period 1963 to 1969.

Let us suppose that we know the quantity of each of the products which constituted the gross domestic product in 1963 and in 1969 and, further, that each product produced in one year was also produced in the other. With these data we could compile a set of quantity ratios expressing the final output of each product in 1969 in terms of the corresponding final output in 1963. The problem then is: how are we to average these ratios? We could simply add them up and divide their sum by the number of final products, but this would not be very satisfactory since a big item like bread would contribute no more to the answer than a small item like birdseed. One way of getting over this difficulty would be to weight the ratio for each product by the relative importance of that product in the total output of 1963. If we added up the weighted ratios and divided by the value of total output in 1963 we should obtain what is called a weighted average of the ratios, to which each ratio would contribute in proportion to the value of the corresponding product in 1963.

Before we go any further let us be quite clear about the type of calculation that has just been described, since it forms the basis of almost all practical comparisons of quantity and price levels over space and time. Consider a community that lives on bread and cheese and keeps pet birds. The entire final product of this community consists of bread, cheese and birdseed. The prices, quantities and values of these three commodities are assumed to have been as follows in two periods which we wish to compare:

	Base period (period 0)			Current period (period 1)		
	Price (£ per ton)	Quantity (tons)	Value (price × quantity)	Price (£ per ton)	Quantity (tons)	Value (price × quantity)
Bread	20	100	2,000	30	90	2,700
Cheese	50	10	500	40	15	600
Birdseed ..	10	10	100	25	20	500
Total			2,600			3,800

The changes in the quantities of the three products relative to period 0 are respectively $90/100 = 0{\cdot}9$, $15/10 = 1{\cdot}5$ and $20/10 = 2{\cdot}0$. If we multiply, or weight, each quantity ratio by the corresponding value in period 0 as shown in the table and add up the resulting numbers, we obtain $(2000 \times 0{\cdot}9) + (500 \times 1{\cdot}5) + (100 \times 2{\cdot}0) = 2750$. If we now divide this sum by the total value in period 0, we obtain $2750/2600 = 1{\cdot}058$ approximately. This is the weighted average of the ratios. We could obtain the numerator even more simply by multiplying the quantities in period 1 by their respective prices in period 0 and adding up the resulting numbers. Thus $(20 \times 90) + (50 \times 15) + (10 \times 20) = 2750$ as before.

Thus, according to this calculation, total product was higher in period 1 than it was in period 0 by 5·8 per cent in *real terms*. That the increase should work out to some such small figure is intuitively plausible since, while the consumption of cheese and birdseed went up considerably, the consumption of bread, which is much the biggest constituent of total product, actually fell by 10 per cent. This shows the importance of weighting; if we had taken a simple average of the quantity ratios we should have obtained $(0{\cdot}9 + 1{\cdot}5 + 2{\cdot}0)/3 = 1{\cdot}467$ approximately, indicating a rise in quantity of 46·7 per cent. This result is absurd, being larger than the rise in the value of total product in spite of the substantial increases in the prices of bread and birdseed.

The obvious comment on the estimate of 5·8 per cent for the rise in total product is that there is no particular reason for using the values of period 0 as weights in preference to the values of period 1. If we did the calculation the other way round we should have to take the sum of the quantities of period 0 each multiplied by its respective price in period 1 and divide this total by the sum of the values in period 1. To compare period 1 with period 0 on this basis we should then have to take the reciprocal of this ratio. This alternative estimate is $3800/[(30 \times 100) + (40 \times 10) + (25 \times 10)] = 1{\cdot}041$. So on this basis the total product of period 1 was only 4·1 per cent higher than the total product of period 0. Since we have no reason to prefer one estimate to the other we might say at this point that the true increase probably lies between 4·1 and 5·8 per cent; and since for practical purposes we shall often want a single figure, we can easily obtain one by averaging the two estimates.

So far we have concentrated on the average change in quantities. Suppose now that we turn our attention to the average change in prices. This can be determined by the same technique which we have applied to quantity changes. And, quite apart from the intrinsic interest of such calculations, we shall see that they also provide an alternative approach to the measurement of quantity changes, since if the change in the total value of product is divided, or 'deflated' by the average price change, the operation will give precisely the quantity measure which we have derived above by a more direct route.

2. *Index-Numbers of Prices and Quantities*

Let us now see why this is so by setting out the formulae we have just described for average changes in quantities and in prices. Estimates based on such formulae are called *index-numbers*. They may take many mathematical forms; those described are called *aggregative index-numbers* and are the most commonly used because they are easy to understand, simple to calculate and possess a number of other convenient properties.

In the conventional symbolism of index-numbers, prices and quantities are denoted respectively by the symbols p and q, to which is added the suffix 0 or 1 according as they relate to the base or to the current period. The usual sign for summation, Σ, is used to denote the sum of the values which constitute a product total. Each of these values has the form of price multiplied by quantity. Thus $\Sigma p_0 q_0$ denotes the sum of base-period quantities each multiplied by its price in the base period, and $\Sigma p_1 q_0$ denotes the sum of base-period quantities each multiplied by its price in the current period. In terms of the numerical example given in the last section, $\Sigma p_1 q_0 = (30 \times 100) + (40 \times 10) + (25 \times 10) = 3650$.

The typical quantity ratio relating the current period to the base period is q_1/q_0. If each such ratio is multiplied by the corresponding value in the base period and if the resulting numbers are added together and divided by the sum of the values in the base period, we obtain

$$\frac{\Sigma\left(p_0 q_0 \cdot \frac{q_1}{q_0}\right)}{\Sigma p_0 q_0} = \frac{\Sigma p_0 q_1}{\Sigma p_0 q_0} \qquad \ldots (1)$$

This is Laspeyres' formula for an index-number of quantities and may be denoted by Q_L. From the left-hand side of (1) this index-number can be regarded as a base-weighted arithmetic average of quantity ratios. From the right-hand side of (1) it can be regarded as the current product total revalued at base-period prices divided by the actual value of the base-period product total.

If in (1) we interchanged the 0's and 1's we should get similar expressions in which the role of base and current periods had been interchanged. If we then took the reciprocals of these expressions we should return to our original base and so should obtain another index-number comparable with (1). It would have the form

$$\frac{\Sigma p_1 q_1}{\Sigma\left(p_1 q_1 \cdot \frac{q_0}{q_1}\right)} = \frac{\Sigma p_1 q_1}{\Sigma p_1 q_0} \qquad \ldots (2)$$

This is Paasche's formula for an index-number of quantities and may be denoted by Q_P. From the left-hand side of (2) this index-number can be regarded as a current-weighted harmonic average of the quantity ratios q_1/q_0. From the right-hand side of (2) it can be regarded as the actual value of the current product total divided by the base product total revalued at current prices.

The formulae in (1) and (2) are measures of the average change in quantities. Corresponding measures of the average change in prices can be obtained by interchanging the p's and q's. Thus from (1) we obtain

$$\frac{\Sigma\left(p_0 q_0 \cdot \frac{p_1}{p_0}\right)}{\Sigma p_0 q_0} = \frac{\Sigma p_1 q_0}{\Sigma p_0 q_0} \qquad \ldots (3)$$

This is Laspeyres' formula for an index-number of prices and may be denoted by P_L. Similarly from (2) we obtain

$$\frac{\Sigma p_1 q_1}{\Sigma \left(p_1 q_1 \cdot \frac{p_0}{p_1} \right)} = \frac{\Sigma p_1 q_1}{\Sigma p_0 q_1} \qquad \ldots (4)$$

This is Paasche's formula for an index-number of prices and may be denoted by P_P. The alternative interpretations of P_L and P_P follow exactly those of Q_L and Q_P.

If we denote by V the ratio of the current to the base product total, that is $\Sigma p_1 q_1 / \Sigma p_0 q_0$, then it is easy to see that

$$P_L Q_P = P_P Q_L = V \qquad \ldots (5)$$

In other words, if properly combined these measures of average price-change and average quantity-change multiply out to the change in value, just as would happen with a single commodity. But to achieve this result the measures must be mixed, one being of type L and the other of type P. Single measures can be obtained on these lines by taking the geometric average of the two price index-numbers as a measure, P_F say, of the average price-change and by taking a similar average, Q_F say, of the two quantity index-numbers. Thus

$$P_F = \sqrt{P_L P_P} \qquad \ldots (6)$$

and

$$Q_F = \sqrt{Q_L Q_P} \qquad \ldots (7)$$

and so, as is easily verified,

$$P_F Q_F = V \qquad \ldots (8)$$

These index-numbers, P_F and Q_F, are Fisher's *ideal index-numbers* for prices and quantities.

If we return for a moment to the numerical example given in the preceding section, we can set out the change in value, V, the three index-numbers of prices, P_L, P_P and P_F, and the three index-numbers of quantities, Q_L, Q_P and Q_F, as follows:

$$V = 1{\cdot}462$$
$$P_L = 1{\cdot}404$$
$$P_P = 1{\cdot}382$$
$$P_F = 1{\cdot}393$$
$$Q_L = 1{\cdot}058$$
$$Q_P = 1{\cdot}041$$
$$Q_F = 1{\cdot}049$$

The reader should have no difficulty in checking these results and in verifying the relationships (5) and (8) above for this example.

Many other forms of index-numbers have been devised. A systematic account of most of them has been given by Fisher in [20] and new suggestions are constantly appearing. However, as we have already said, the above forms are simple and convenient and we shall not go beyond them.

3. *Measures of Individual Prices and Quantities*

We have seen that the comparisons we can make are affected numerically by the formula used, but so long as we rely on well-established types of index-number we can be confident that in practice we shall not obtain freakish and misleading results. We have also seen that our comparisons are affected by the choice of base year. In actual cases this choice will often be determined by practical considerations such as the availability of data or the desire for comparability with other series. But, in so far as we have a choice, we should remember that relative prices stand for relative valuations by consumers or producers and we should therefore try to choose a period when these are normal. This means that we should try to avoid a year which contains a general strike, a failure of the harvest or the onset of a depression because we may expect that in such years many markets will be seriously out of equilibrium so that relative prices and relative quantities will be unrepresentative.

With a little care, therefore, these problems are not serious.

The real difficulty in constructing index-numbers is to obtain enough accurate information on the movement of individual prices and quantities.

We have seen that the data needed to construct price index-numbers are the same as are needed to construct quantity index-numbers and so in the following brief account we shall concentrate on the latter. In order to compare total product in two years we must subdivide the total value according to products and measure the quantity change of each component. Most of the information readily available on quantities is expressed in simple units such as number, weight, volume or area. But these simple units often mask a considerable diversity in quality, model and other characteristics which affect prices and costs. They ought therefore to be scrutinized very carefully. In doing this the guiding principle to be followed is that similar articles which sell at different prices are *prima facie* different; if further scrutiny confirms this assumption, they should be either treated separately or measured in units such that the prices per unit of the different varieties are approximately equal to one another. Let us look at some typical problems in the light of this principle.

(1) *Quality differences.* Consider the case of eggs, by which we mean hens' eggs. These are usually graded by size and freshness, and different grades sell at different prices. Now, eggs are usually recorded by number. This is a satisfactory indicator of quantity only when there has been no change between the periods under comparison in the average size and freshness of the eggs sold, but when there has been a change we should like it to be reflected in the comparison. If from the available statistics we could distinguish between eggs of different grades, we could treat each grade as a separate commodity, weight it by its own price and everything would be straightforward. Unfortunately the basic data are most unlikely to be available in this detail, but sample information or even the impressions of poultry keepers and distributors may enable us to adjust the crude quantity comparison, provided we

know the relationship between price and quality in the base period.

Another example is provided by beer. In this country the quantity of beer is measured in bulk barrels, which reflect the amount of liquid, and standard barrels, which reflect the amount of alcohol. If the beer becomes stronger, the standard measure will rise more than the bulk measure. Typically the statistics give two totals for the whole output of beer, one in bulk and the other in standard barrels, without distinguishing among different qualities, so that we cannot treat beers of different strengths as separate commodities. But we can work out the relationship between price and strength in the base period and this will tell us how best to combine the two quantity indicators we have. Incidentally, if we have to choose one unit or the other there can be no doubt that we should choose standard barrels.

(2) *New models.* In the case of many manufactured goods, quality changes are introduced to the public by means of new models, with the consequence that similar products made in different years are different. A good example of this are motor-cars. These are typically recorded by number. But their performance, economy, reliability and comfort change very much from period to period as new models are thought up. In principle we could find out how these characteristics were related to price in the base period and then adjust the crude measure in numbers according to the changes that have taken place in these characteristics. In practice, however, it is difficult to compare periods which are not close together: in order to price modern cars at 1910 values it would be necessary to extrapolate the price-quality relationship of 1910 beyond the ranges of quality that were then available. As a short cut we might note the fact that generally speaking the price of cars within each period is closely related to their weight. Thus even a rough estimate in tons would be superior to an accurate estimate in numbers, because most of the desirable features of a car are positively associated with weight. But new technical

developments may change this, and so weight may become a misleading substitute for the qualities that affect price.

(3) *Composite products and fixed charges.* This problem is well illustrated by the case of goods transport. The volume of traffic is usually recorded in ton-miles with some subdivision by commodity. Ton-miles are frequently taken as the quantity indicator for goods transport, but in fact charges are not as a rule proportional to ton-miles since the goods have to be loaded and unloaded, an expense which is independent of distance and in some cases quite considerable. The relationship between the total charge per ton and the distance makes it possible to disentangle the constant part of the charge from the part which varies with distance. The former should be associated with a quantity indicator expressed in tons and the latter with one expressed in ton-miles. If we assume that the total charge per ton is equal to a fixed charge independent of distance plus a constant rate per mile multiplied by distance, we can see that if the fixed charge is zero then we need only an indicator expressed in ton-miles; while if the rate per mile is zero, so that the total charge is independent of distance, then we need only an indicator expressed in tons.

The same idea can be applied to passenger travel, with the number of passengers taking the place of tons of merchandise. We may find that the charge per passenger is a fixed sum independent of distance and in this case the proper quantity indicator is the number of passengers. Or the charge per passenger may be proportional to distance and in this case the proper quantity indicator is the number of passenger-miles. From this we see that the proper indicator depends on the structure of the charges in operation. If this structure changes between the two periods, then the indicator to be used will be that proper to the base period.

The same situation arises when charges are made under a two-part tariff, as frequently happens, for instance, with electricity. In these cases the consumer pays a fixed charge plus a constant charge per unit of current. Electricity consumption is usually measured in units of current (kilowatt-hours), but it would be better if the total expenditure on fixed charges were associated with an indicator of the number of consumers and only the balance of the expenditure were associated with an indicator of the quantity of current consumed.

(4) *Trade and transport charges.* Some farm products, like fresh vegetables, may be consumed by the growers or they may be taken to city markets and sold at prices far exceeding those received by the growers, the difference being made up of trade and transport charges. Accordingly, farm consumption and city consumption should be kept separate because the price per ton is appreciably different in the two cases.

It is sometimes argued that this is all wrong because a cabbage is a cabbage whether it is consumed by a farmer or a townsman and that if anything it is rather more of a cabbage, and so should be weighted more heavily, if it is consumed by a farmer, because in that case it is likely to be fresher. But this argument overlooks the fact that people choose to live in towns and that transport and distributive services are necessary to make this possible. If between two periods there has been a move from country to town, we must recognize the fact that in the later period the community has chosen to devote rather more resources to trade and transport and rather less to growing cabbages, and we should allow this fact to be reflected in our comparison of final product. Although we shall not go into such details here, it can be seen from [46] how it is possible to set out the calculations so as to show in what measure cabbages, trade and transport contribute respectively to the change in final product as a whole.

(5) *Seasonal variations.* Seasonal commodities provide another example of similar goods selling at widely different prices. During their season, strawberries are cheap and consumed in large quantities; out of season they are very expensive and very few are consumed, or they may be altogether unobtainable. The question now is: is a strawberry always a strawberry or are winter strawberries a different commodity

from summer ones? According to the guiding principle of this section they are undoubtedly different commodities. This means that we should not treat the annual consumption of strawberries as a single component of final product with a single average price but we should try to treat strawberries consumed in different seasons as different commodities, each with its own average price. The seasons can be grouped in any way provided that the price within a season is relatively constant. If a single annual indicator is required for the quantity of strawberries consumed, the appropriate one is the sum of the quantities in each season of the current year each multiplied by the normal seasonal level of strawberry prices in the base year divided by the corresponding quantities in the base year each multiplied by the same factor.

Of course if the seasonal pattern of consumption does not change between the two periods under comparison, these more refined calculations will give the same result as crude ones. But in fact the seasonal pattern does change, partly because with rising incomes people can afford more 'out of season' varieties and partly because technical developments such as refrigeration are constantly at work to reduce the price and so increase the consumption of 'out of season' varieties. The effect of such technical progress shows in the refined calculations but not in the crude ones: in all cases where seasonal luxuries have come down in price the consequent rise in consumption will appear higher when weighted by the prices of the earlier period than when weighted by those of the later period.

(6) *Bewildering variety*. In some cases individual articles are produced in a bewildering number of qualities and types and the materials and designs used are constantly changing. Clothing illustrates this problem well. Let us take two simple examples, men's shirts and women's stockings. We might be able to discover the number of shirts bought in each period to be compared, but this would be a crude indicator of quantity since there might have been important changes in quality. If we tried to divide shirts into different categories we should prob-

ably find that the information was not available, and even if it were we should have to face the difficulty that some of the categories did not exist in the base period.

The best thing to do in such cases is to approach the measurement of quantity change through the construction of price index-numbers. In doing this we should concentrate on pricing certain specific articles defined as narrowly as possible in terms of quality, and rely on the fact that goods made of similar materials and by similar processes would probably move in price in approximately the same way as the articles we had chosen as samples. Then by measuring the change in expenditure and dividing it by the price index we might hope to get an improved measure for the change in quantity. For instance, if shirts are either relatively cheap cotton ones or relatively expensive silk ones, the price index might show no change, the total number of shirts bought might show no change either, but the expenditure on shirts might have increased: this would indicate that people were now buying relatively more silk shirts and relatively fewer cotton ones than in the base period, in other words that the average quality of shirts had risen, a fact which would be reflected in the ratio of the change in expenditure to the change in the price index-number.

It must be remembered that in practice difficulties are seldom encountered singly, and it may well happen that some of the difficulties discussed above will be superimposed on the problem of bewildering variety. Thus a change in raw materials may make it very hard to continue a price series of constant quality because the popular article selected for pricing in the base year has been largely replaced by a similar article with different characteristics. The substitution of nylon stockings for silk ones is a case in point: if a pair of nylon stockings lasts perceptibly longer than a pair of silk ones, then the pair ceases to be a satisfactory unit and we are back at the problem discussed at (2) above.

This summary of the difficulties of defining suitable units leaves many questions unanswered. A fuller treatment will be found in the O.E.E.C. report on index-numbers [46] which has already been referred to, and in [76]. The only thing to be added here is that it is from attention to basic details of the kind discussed in this section more than from debates on formulae or base periods that improvements are likely to come.

4. *Final Product and Value Added at Constant Prices*

So far, the product totals we have had in mind have been totals of final product, namely the gross domestic product and its components. Before we leave this field we should recall our earlier discussion of the production boundary in which we decided to put all activity in households and government outside that boundary, with a small number of specific exceptions. When we come to quantity comparisons this means that the quantities we are trying to measure for these sectors are the quantities of goods and services, including the direct services of labour, which households and government departments buy. This in turn means that the final product associated with, say, education is to be measured in real terms by references to what goes into education and we do not have to consider what comes out of it any more than we have to consider what households do with food, string, paper hats and all the other things they buy.

At first sight this may seem unsatisfactory but reflection will show that it is less unsatisfactory than the practicable alternatives. For how should we construct a quantity indicator for education? Should we take the number of students, or the total number of marks gained in national examinations, or what? Any such measure would be inferior to a measure based on inputs since, despite Parkinson and his law, there can be no doubt that more teachers, larger class rooms, more equipment and greater facilities give us the best approximation we can get to more education; it may not be a very good one but it is better than the number of students or the number of marks.

We have already seen that, for the economy as a whole, total final product is identically equal to total value added.

This is evident in table 2 above, the upper half of which shows the different categories of final product while the lower half shows the components of total value added. These components could be subdivided by industry and then added together industry-wise to give total value added in each industry. These industrial values added are composed of primary inputs, depreciation and indirect taxes, or of primary inputs alone if we value final products at factor cost and net.

Suppose now that we try to compare the value of primary inputs in terms of constant prices. We might approach this problem by trying to find quantity indicators for primary inputs, but once we had done the calculation for labour we should find the other factors of production, namely capital and land, much more difficult to handle. In fact little has been done so far in this field, but if the calculation could be made it would provide a measure of the quantity of primary inputs which when divided into the quantity of output would show the change in productivity of all primary inputs taken together.

There is, however, an entirely different approach which allows the whole calculation to be carried out by revaluing products. Value added is the excess of the value of an industry's output over the value of the intermediate products, which we shall here call intermediate inputs, consumed by that industry. If the quantities in the current period are all revalued at the prices of the base period and if, for each industry, the revalued intermediate inputs are subtracted from the revalued output, there results a set of measures of value added at base-period prices which can be compared with the actual values added in the base period.

This measure of value added at constant prices corresponds to value added as net output rather than as primary input. The interesting thing is that if values added at base-period prices are summed over all industries the same figure is reached as when final products at base-period prices are summed over all industries. The reason for this is not difficult to see: starting with the total value of output in each industry, to get final product we subtract that part of the industry's output which goes to other industries (its output of intermediate product), and to get value added we subtract in each case the product of other industries which goes to the industry in question (its input of intermediate product). When we sum these calculations over all industries we have in each case the value of all goods and services produced *less* the value of all intermediate product. This identity is true whatever prices are used and so the domestic product account balances at constant as well as at current prices. We may therefore show the gross domestic product at constant prices either as the sum of all final products emerging from the productive system or as the sum of all values added in the different branches of production.

In principle, the value-added calculation as we have described it is that used for index-numbers of industrial production except that it is extended to all forms of activity within the production boundary. In practice, when constructing an index-number of industrial production it is usual to assume that an industry's intermediate inputs are proportional to its output, and so the value added in each industry is multiplied by a single indicator of quantity change. Further details on this subject can be found in [65].

5. *Total Product at Constant Prices: Britain*

Let us now return to the *Blue Book* and see how these comparisons work out in practice. Table 12 shows, for selected years, the course of the gross domestic product at constant prices over the period 1938 to 1969. This table is based on estimates of final product: the upper panel shows the money totals for the various years recalculated at 1963 prices; and the lower panel shows the same figures expressed as index-numbers with 1963 = 100. The figures in the lower panel, though they give no indication of the magnitude of the different series, make it easier to take in their movements over time and to compare these movements.

TABLE 12

Gross Domestic Product at Constant (1963) Values
United Kingdom
(1963 £ million; 1963 = 100)

	1938*	1948*	1954*	1959	1963	1964	1965	1966	1967	1968	1969
1. Gross domestic product at market prices: final product based on expenditure data	**17,749**	**19,968**	**23,800**	**26,611**	**30,245**	**31,932**	**32,685**	**33,385**	**34,071**	**35,235**	**35,794**
(*a*) Consumers' expenditure											
(i) Private	13,486	13,808	15,447	17,747	20,087	20,783	21,183	21,623	22,075	22,589	22,681
(ii) Public	2,908	3,883	4,944	4,668	5,184	5,272	5,418	5,562	5,855	5,875	5,814
(*b*) Gross domestic investment											
(i) Fixed assets ..	2,495	2,285	3,191	4,025	4,907	5,720	5,949	6,100	6,505	6,865	6,682
(ii) Stocks	0	241	52	188	198	640	385	254	184	157	357
(*c*) Exports	2,700	3,248	4,393	5,045	5,815	6,018	6,306	6,561	6,572	7,380	8,052
(*d*) *less* Imports	–3,787	–3,449	–4,155	–5,062	–5,946	–6,501	–6,556	–6,715	–7,120	–7,631	–7,792
2. Index-numbers of gross domestic product at market prices	**59**	**66**	**79**	**88**	**100**	**106**	**108**	**110**	**113**	**116**	**118**
(*a*) Consumers' expenditure											
(i) Private	67	69	77	88	100	103	105	108	110	112	113
(ii) Public	56	75	95	90	100	102	105	107	113	113	112
(*b*) Gross domestic investment†	49	49	64	83	100	125	124	124	131	138	138
(*c*) Exports	46	56	76	87	100	103	108	113	113	127	138
(*d*) Imports	64	58	70	85	100	109	110	113	120	128	131

* In these years the components in the top part of the table do not sum exactly to the total for the reason indicated on p. 104.
† Includes investment in stocks. For fixed assets alone the series is: 51, 47, 65, 82, 100, 117, 121, 124, 133, 140, 136.

Between 1948 and 1969 the gross domestic product at constant market prices rose by 79 per cent, which implies an average annual increase of 2·8 per cent. This average, however, was not realized every year: there were great spurts in 1952–55, 1958–61, 1962–64 and 1967–68 and in between the rate of increase was much lower; compared with the inter-war period, the postwar years are characterized by fluctuations of comparatively small amplitude and comparatively high frequency.

The postwar figures up to 1964 in table 12 come from table 14 of the *Blue Book*; and those from 1965 onwards embody the revisions contained in the issue of *Economic Trends* for April 1971. Recently, the year taken as the basis for valuation has been changed from 1958 to 1963. The estimates for the years from 1963 to date have been calculated in detail in relation to the new base year. Those for 1958 to 1962 have been less fully recalculated and form a coherent system linked to 1963. Those for 1948 to 1957 are simply the earlier estimates linked to the new series at the level of detail shown in the *Blue Book*. Those for 1938 are the estimates given in the preceding edition of this book similarly linked to the new series in 1958. As a consequence of these procedures the estimates for 1938, 1948 and 1954 do not form completely coherent sets, although the discrepancies between the totals and the sums of the components are not very large.

If we want to know how the different industries contributed to movements in the gross domestic product we can find the answer in the top part of table 13. This table is based on relative factor costs and not on relative market prices, as was table 12. Rises well above the average took place in several branches of manufacturing industry, notably chemicals, in public utilities and in the insurance and banking group. Rises around the average took place in agriculture, construction and transport. Lowest of all we find mining and quarrying, which declined during the war and never regained its prewar level, and public administration and defence.

The postwar estimates based on output data are taken from

TABLE 13

Index-Numbers of Gross Domestic Product at Constant (1963) Values
United Kingdom
(*1963 = 100*)

	1938	1948	1954	1959	1963	1964	1965	1966	1967	1968	1969
1. Gross domestic product at factor cost: value added based on output data	**61**	**68**	**80**	**89**	**100**	**106**	**109**	**111**	**112**	**117**	**119**
(a) Agriculture, forestry and fishing	59	67	81	87	100	104	107	107	111	112	112
(b) Mining and quarrying	120	101	112	103	100	100	96	90	89	85	80
(c) Food, drink and tobacco	60	70	80	90	100	103	105	109	111	116	119
(d) Chemicals and allied industries	26	43	63	80	100	110	117	123	130	140	149
(e) Metal manufacture	50	73	88	93	100	113	118	111	104	111	115
(f) Engineering and allied industries	37	55	75	88	100	109	113	116	116	122	127
(g) Textiles, leather and clothing	95	85	97	96	100	105	108	107	103	113	116
(h) Other manufacturing	50	54	76	86	100	112	114	115	117	124	126
(i) Construction	78	68	79	87	100	111	114	115	119	122	119
(j) Gas, electricity and water	29	44	63	77	100	105	112	117	121	128	136
(k) Transport and communication	56	72	83	89	100	106	108	110	112	115	119
(l) Distributive trades	71	65	78	90	100	103	106	107	108	111	112
(m) Insurance, banking, finance and business services	58	58	69	86	100	105	108	112	118	127	133
(n) Ownership of dwellings	74	80	84	93	100	102	104	107	111	114	117
(o) Professional and scientific services	56	62	76	89	100	103	107	111	114	119	123
(p) Miscellaneous services	105	85	81	88	100	105	106	107	107	108	108
(q) Public administration and defence	72	109	110	99	100	100	101	104	107	106	105
2. Gross domestic product at factor cost: value added based on income data	..	**66**	**79**	**87**	**100**	**106**	**109**	**111**	**112**	**116**	**118**
3. Gross domestic product at factor cost: final product based on expenditure data	**57**	**66**	**79**	**88**	**100**	**105**	**108**	**110**	**112**	**116**	**117**

table 15 of the *Blue Book*. In the lower part of table 13 we find alternative index-numbers of the gross domestic product at factor cost which are taken from table 8 of the *Blue Book*. By comparing rows 1, 2 and 3 we can see the extent to which these largely independent estimates, though agreeing in their general movement, show small discrepancies as measures of year-to-year changes. By comparing row 3 of table 13 with row 2 of table 12 we can see the small differences made by taking factor costs rather than market prices as the basis for valuation.

Tables 12 and 13 express quantity changes. If we want to use them to measure price changes we must divide the entries that interest us into the corresponding figures at current values. Let us assume, for instance, that we want to measure the average price change between 1954 and 1969. Taking the measures based on expenditure data, we can see from table 12 that at 1963 prices the gross domestic product rose from £23,800 million to £35,794 million; and if we go back to table 1, we can see that at current market prices it rose during the same period from £17,760 million to £45,174 million, the latter figure being revised to £45,465 million in the issue of *Economic Trends* for April 1971. Accordingly, (45,465/35,794)/(17,760/23,800) = 1·70 indicates a rise in prices of 70 per cent between 1954 and 1969 as measured by a Paasche index-number of prices with 1963 = 100.

Similarly, if we want to derive this price change from index-numbers, we must first put the current values for the 1954 and 1969 totals in index-number form, with 1963 = 100, and then divide them by the corresponding figures in table 12. Thus at current prices the gross domestic product rose from 59 in 1954 to 100 in 1963 and 150 in 1969; at 1963 prices the corresponding figures were 79, 100 and 118. The implicit price series is therefore 59/79 = 0·75, 100/100 = 1 and 150/118 = 1·27. And 1·27/0·75 = 1·69 which, allowing for rounding-off errors, is the same percentage as we reached above.

By now the point of these calculations should be clear. Between 1954 and 1969 the gross domestic product increased in money terms from £17,760 million to £45,465 million, that is to say by 156 per cent. By making index-numbers of quantities and prices we see that in real terms it rose in fact by about 50 per cent and the rest of the increase was only apparent, being due to a rise of about 70 per cent in prices. This is a big step forward in our analysis of economic events, though we must always remember that if we had reversed the roles of Laspeyres and Paasche or had chosen the relative values of a different year our answers would have been slightly different.

6. *Total Product at Constant Prices: America*

The course of the real product totals in America is set out in table 14 below. The estimates are based on table 1.2 and 1.6 of the *Survey*, with adjustments in respect of exports and imports made with the help of information not available in the *Survey*. These adjustments are necessary because the Americans record only national, and not domestic, totals. It will be noticed that the American figures are based on 1958 rather than on 1963, as was the case with the British ones.

The first thing we see from table 14 is the great increase in American productive activity over the war period: between 1938 and 1948 their gross domestic product rose by 68 per cent (or 5·2 per cent per annum) as opposed to 13 per cent (or 1·2 per cent per annum) in Britain. After the war the rate of growth, though still faster than in Britain, slowed down somewhat: over the twenty-one years between 1948 and 1969 the total increase was 124 per cent (or 3·8 per cent per annum).

The components of the gross domestic product too followed a very different course from that of their British counterparts: between 1948 and 1969, private consumption rose by 122 per cent; public consumption by 218 per cent; investment in fixed assets by 100 per cent; exports by 149 per cent; and imports by 285 per cent. Thus while in Britain consumption rose more slowly and investment much faster than product, in America the position was reversed, which at first sight would suggest a rather happy-go-lucky attitude towards investment.

TABLE 14

Gross Domestic Product at Constant (1958) Values
United States
(1958 $ milliard; 1958 = 100)

	1938	1948	1954	1959	1963	1964	1965	1966	1967	1968	1969
1. Gross domestic product at market prices: final product based on expenditure data	**191·8**	**322·5**	**405·4**	**473·8**	**547·6**	**577·0**	**613·7**	**654·1**	**670·8**	**702·7**	**723·1**
(*a*) Consumers' expenditure ..											
(i) Private	140·2	210·8	255·7	307·3	353·3	373·7	397·7	418·1	430·1	452·3	467·7
(ii) Public	27·5	40·4	75·7	78·6	91·8	92·8	95·6	106·8	120·2	127·8	128·4
(*b*) Gross domestic investment											
(i) Fixed assets	25·8	61·8	74·6	84·9	94·5	100·3	109·2	115·1	113·5	119·3	123·5
(ii) Stocks	–2·4	4·6	–2·0	4·8	5·8	5·8	9·0	13·9	7·7	6·9	7·2
(*c*) Exports	8·3	16·6	16·8	21·1	27·9	31·6	32·2	34·8	36·2	39·2	41·3
(*d*) *less* Imports	–7·6	–11·7	–15·4	–22·9	–25·7	–27·2	–30·0	–34·6	–36·9	–42·8	–45·0
2. Index-numbers of gross domestic product at market prices ..	**43**	**72**	**91**	**106**	**123**	**130**	**138**	**147**	**151**	**158**	**162**
(*a*) Consumers' expenditure ..											
(i) Private	48	73	88	106	122	129	137	144	148	156	161
(ii) Public	35	51	96	100	117	118	122	136	153	163	164
(*b*) Gross domestic investment*	31	87	95	117	131	139	154	168	158	165	171
(*c*) Exports	40	81	82	102	135	153	156	169	176	190	200
(*d*) Imports	37	57	75	112	126	133	147	170	181	210	221

* Includes investment in stocks. For fixed assets only the series is: 33, 79, 96, 109, 121, 128, 140, 147, 145, 153, 158.

Before we jump to any such conclusion, however, we shall be wise to go back to what we said on p. 38 about investment as a percentage of total product. From tables 12 and 14 we see that at constant prices the ratio of fixed investment to gross domestic product in 1938 was 14 per cent in Britain and over 13 per cent in America; in 1948 it was over 11 per cent in Britain and 19 per cent in America; and in 1969 it was nearly 19 per cent in Britain and over 17 per cent in America. This puts the course of events in better perspective: America, less strained by the war, had reached by 1948 a high ratio of investment to product, which dropped only slightly in recent years; in Britain this ratio in 1948 was still relatively low, and it was only in the 1960's that it managed to catch up with the American percentage and eventually overtake it.

Another point to bear in mind is that in all the comparisons we have made so far we have only discussed the growth of the two economies as collective units and have not considered how this growth affected the individuals within these units. For this purpose the first thing to do is to put these comparisons on a per head basis. Between 1948 and 1969 the gross domestic product of Britain rose by 79 per cent, that of America by 124 per cent; at the same time the population of Britain increased from 49·6 to 55·6 million, that of America from 147·2 to 202·6 million. Thus the gross domestic product *per head of the population* rose by 60 per cent (or 2·2 per cent per annum) in Britain and 63 per cent (or 2·3 per cent per annum) in America.

As usual, however, this first conclusion, though correct in a sense and quite useful, is too simple. What does 'per head' mean? The large increase in the American population consists partly of an increase in the proportion of babies and young children, who do not consume so much product as adults do: if more cars are produced, this does not mean that the new generations of Americans go to their kindergarten driving their Cadillacs, but that their parents can now afford two cars instead of one. To pursue these calculations to a great degree of refinement is impossible without investigating the age distribution of the population and the relative capacity for consumption of the different age groups. In this short book we shall not go into these matters. We have only mentioned them here as another example of how careful one has to be in order to make valid comparisons.

7. *Quarterly Series*

As we said at the end of Chapter I, nowadays both Britain and America produce a large number of quarterly statistics which enable the national accounts to be kept up to date. For Britain the quarterly series appear in the October, January, April and July numbers of *Economic Trends* [60] and are keyed in to the annual estimates given in September of each year in the *Blue Book*. These series go back to 1955 and cover most aspects of the national accounts, though in much less detail than the *Blue Book* does; in particular, there are no quarterly figures for depreciation, so that the estimates of income, product, saving and investment exist only on a gross basis. Although most of the series are expressed only at current values, those for final product and its main components are also expressed at constant values.

Similar information for America can be found in the *Survey*.

When one passes from annual to quarterly series a new difficulty arises in making valid comparisons: quarterly series are, to a greater or lesser extent, subject to seasonal influences which obscure their underlying trend. This is not the place in which to embark on a lengthy description of the problems of seasonal adjustment; a discussion of many of the issues, both conceptual and practical, can be found in [40; 50, pp. 57–72]. Nevertheless a few words on the subject, in addition to what was said in section 3 above, may be useful.

If we draw a graph of a quarterly (or monthly) economic series, we usually find that it exhibits visible fluctuations from season to season, which more or less repeat themselves year after year. For example, if we take consumers' expenditure in

Britain we find that as a rule it is about 4 per cent below trend during the first quarter, very close to trend during the second and third quarters and about 4 per cent above trend during the last quarter. Such variations, which of course differ greatly from one series to another, are due to a large number of causes: climatic conditions, such as temperature, rainfall and sunshine; the vagaries of the calendar, such as the incidence of normal working days and movable feasts; and human responses to these factors, such as the fixing of holiday periods and the discontinuities that arise in production from, say, the difference between summer and winter clothing. Some of these factors are constant and produce constant seasonal patterns: Christmas comes at the same time every year and with it the demand for turkeys and small fir trees soars. Some change gradually and the patterns change gradually with them: as more and more employers grant holidays with pay, more and more people take summer holidays and more and more establishments have to close down during that season. Finally, some are irregular and produce irregularities in the patterns: a late warm Easter will send record crowds to the seaside; a very cold winter will lead to an abnormally high consumption of fuel.

With so many influences at work some kind of strategy is needed in approaching the problem of seasonal adjustment. In the first place, although most economic series follow a seasonal pattern, it should not be too readily assumed that all do, since not all variations have seasonal causes: wars, changes of government, movements of population, fashions are not seasonal phenomena, yet they too may produce noticeable peaks and troughs in a series. The first step, therefore, is to try to decide whether the variations in a series are due to seasonal influences or not.

For this purpose we need not consider seasonal factors; the clue lies in the pattern formed by the observations themselves. In order to find out what this pattern is like, we must first fit a trend to the series as a whole, so that the observations can be expressed as deviations from the trend; if we then group these deviations by season and calculate each season's average, we can see (i) what the position of the individual observations is in relation to their respective averages and (ii) what the position of the averages is in relation to each other. If the underlying seasonal pattern is stable, one of four situations will emerge from these calculations. First, the seasonal averages may be widely dispersed but the observations for each season may show little dispersion from their average. In this case there is a well-marked constant seasonal pattern and by removing it a smooth adjusted series will be obtained. Second, at the opposite extreme, the seasonal averages may be very alike but the observations for each season may show a wide dispersion around their average. In this case there would be little to be gained by seasonal adjustment since the average differences between seasons are small and uncertain. Third, the seasonal averages may be very alike and the observations for each season may cluster closely round them. In this case the original series will itself be smooth and, while it is possible to estimate a seasonal pattern, the series will not be much changed by its removal. Finally, the seasonal averages may be very different from one another and the observations for each season may show a wide dispersion around their average. In this case there is a seasonal pattern to be observed but it cannot be determined accurately. If it is removed, the result will not be a smooth series but one in which successive observations are distributed more at random than they were originally.

Having decided that an adjustment is required, the next step is to consider how to carry it out. This depends on whether the seasonal pattern we have found is constant or shows signs of gradual change from year to year. In the first case we can eliminate the seasonal variations by removing from each observation the relevant seasonal average, or seasonal constant. In the second case we must replace these constants by variables which change gradually with time. These variables, however, must be regularly re-examined, since even small monotonic movements will produce in time a substantial alteration in the seasonal pattern and cannot therefore be expected to persist for long with undiminished vigour. This method, which is an application of the analysis of variance and covariance, is explained in detail and exemplified in [50, pp. 57–72].

So far we have tried, more or less mechanically, to associate with each season a regular deviation, either constant or slowly changing, from the trend, without considering what factors lie behind these deviations. The third step is to examine such factors and see how far they may account for irregularities in the pattern. For example, a normal pattern shows a higher consumption of fuel in winter than in summer; we know that this is due to temperature; so we may legitimately conclude that if in one winter the consumption of fuel was abnormally high this was most probably due to an abnormally cold season. This may seem painfully obvious. But the fact is that in tracing such connections a good deal of care is needed, for various reasons. Thus abnormality in a given factor may not have consistent effects in all seasons: an abnormally cold winter will indeed lead to an abnormally high consumption of fuel, but an abnormally hot summer cannot lead to an abnormally low consumption of fuel if no fuel is used for heating in normal summers; on the contrary, if a substantial number of the buildings in a country are air-conditioned, an abnormally hot summer will lead to an abnormally high consumption of fuel for cooling. Also, different factors, such as temperature and sunshine, are correlated, so that their effects may be hard to disentangle. Because of these and other pitfalls the third step, finding the causes of seasonal irregularities, is much the most laborious and not unnaturally statisticians tend very often to stop short of it.

However far we go in attempting to adjust a series for seasonal variations, the object is the same; to get a better estimate of the underlying movements of the series, undisturbed by purely seasonal factors. Examples of quarterly series before and after adjustment are given in tables 15 and 16. These tables, which are derived from the April 1971 issue of *Economic*

TAB

Unadjusted Quarterly Series of Gr
Uni
(19

	1968			
	i	ii	iii	iv
Gross domestic product at market prices: final product based on expenditure data	**8,549**	**8,649**	**8,759**	**9,2**
(*a*) Consumers' expenditure				
(i) Private	5,512	5,562	5,605	5,9
(ii) Public	1,514	1,451	1,444	1,4
(*b*) Gross domestic investment				
(i) Fixed assets	1,753	1,601	1,670	1,8
(ii) Stocks	−122	120	111	
(*c*) Exports	1,804	1,810	1,865	1,9
(*d*) *less* Imports	−1,912	−1,895	−1,936	−1,8

TAB

Seasonally Adjusted Quarterly Series of Gr
Uni
(19

	1968			
	i	ii	iii	iv
Gross domestic product at market prices: final product based on expenditure data	**8,751**	**8,657**	**8,830**	**8,9**
(*a*) Consumers' expenditure				
(i) Private	5,769	5,546	5,621	5,6
(ii) Public	1,487	1,467	1,470	1,4
(*b*) Gross domestic investment				
(i) Fixed assets	1,705	1,678	1,695	1,7
(ii) Stocks	−119	71	88	1
(*c*) Exports	1,823	1,772	1,873	1,9
(*d*) *less* Imports	−1,914	−1,877	−1,917	−1,9

5

omestic Product at Constant (1963) Values
ingdom
million)

1969				1970			
i	ii	iii	iv	i	ii	iii	iv
3,519	**8,918**	**8,947**	**9,410**	**8,701**	**9,137**	**9,075**	**9,576**
5,352	5,684	5,668	5,977	5,480	5,828	5,873	6,161
1,483	1,427	1,431	1,473	1,495	1,463	1,462	1,480
1,678	1,589	1,668	1,747	1,669	1,661	1,676	1,771
99	119	71	68	−37	159	132	97
1,837	2,056	2,075	2,084	2,038	2,147	2,002	2,180
1,930	−1,957	−1,966	−1,939	−1,944	−2,121	−2,070	−2,113

omestic Product at Constant (1963) Values
ingdom
million)

1969				1970			
i	ii	iii	iv	i	ii	iii	iv
3,727	**8,930**	**9,032**	**9,105**	**8,884**	**9,162**	**9,174**	**9,269**
5,588	5,678	5,691	5,724	5,720	5,819	5,895	5,908
1,455	1,445	1,457	1,457	1,467	1,480	1,487	1,466
1,640	1,661	1,692	1,689	1,631	1,736	1,698	1,712
96	84	51	126	−31	106	117	159
1,887	2,002	2,077	2,086	2,090	2,094	2,004	2,179
1,939	−1,940	−1,936	−1,977	−1,993	−2,073	−2,027	−2,155

Trends, show the quarterly course of the gross domestic product and its main components in Britain from the beginning of 1968 to the end of 1970, and are directly comparable with the upper part of table 12: for each series, the sum of the four quarters in each year in either table is equal to the total for that year given in table 12. Similar tables could be compiled for America from the *Survey*; but they would not be fully comparable with the annual figures given in table 14 because American quarterly information on foreign transactions is not detailed enough to enable us to separate imports and exports from factor incomes paid abroad and received from abroad.

The contrast between adjusted and unadjusted quarterly movements, and between these and annual movements, can be seen more clearly still in diagram 2. This diagram is constructed partly from table 12 and partly from tables 15 and 16. Each series starts in 1963 and ends in 1970. The period 1963–67 is shown as an annual run, the period 1968–70 as a twofold quarterly run, the dotted lines indicating the pattern formed by the actual observations, the solid lines the pattern that emerges after seasonal adjustment. The points representing the annual figures have been brought down to a quarterly level by dividing each year's total by four. Visually, these points are placed in mid-year, while those representing the quarterly figures are placed in mid-quarter; hence the gap between 1967 and the first quarter of 1968. The scales for the individual series alternate between left and right; thus the scale for imports, which goes from £1,400 million to £2,200 million, is the lowest on the left; that for exports, which also goes from £1,400 million to £2,200 million, is the next up on the right; that for investment in fixed assets, which goes from £1,200 million to £1,800 million, is again on the left; and so on. Product levels are measured on a logarithmic or ratio scale, which means that a given vertical distance represents a given proportionate difference and not a given absolute one; thus the distance separating 1,000 from 1,200 is the same as that separating 5,000 from 6,000. On this scale an upward-sloping

DIAGRAM 2

Gross Domestic Product and its Components United Kingdom (*1963 £ million*)

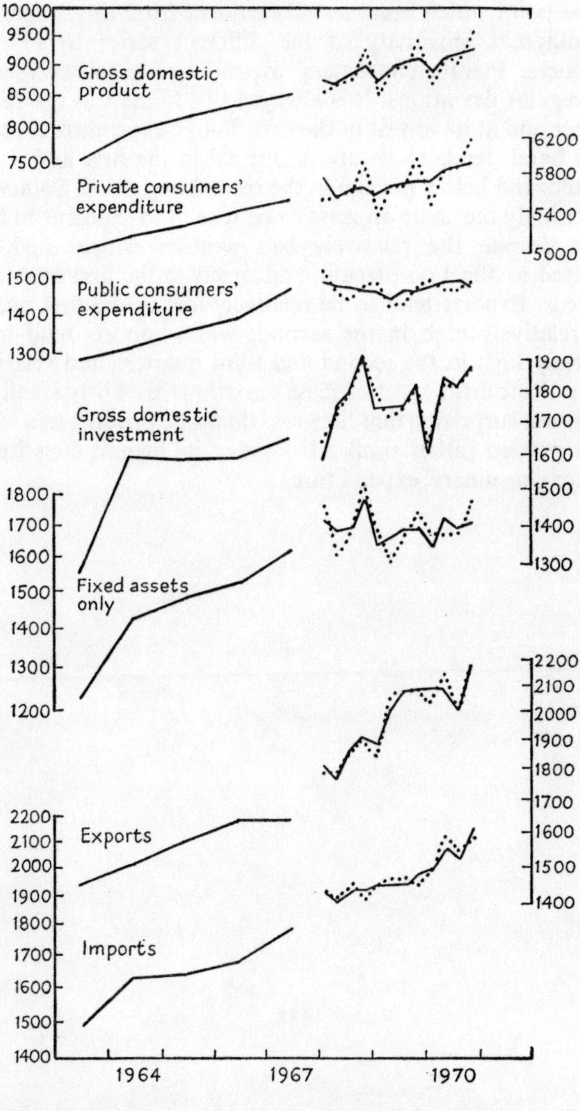

line corresponds to a constant proportionate rate of growth over time.

One point which becomes very evident from this diagram is the different sensitivity of the different series to seasonal influences. Private consumers' expenditure has very marked and regular deviations: it is always at its highest in the fourth quarter and at its lowest in the first. Public expenditure, on the other hand, tends to be above normal in the first and fourth quarters and below normal in the second and third. Somewhat surprisingly the same appears to be true of investment in fixed assets despite the relatively bad weather which might be expected to affect construction adversely in the first quarter of the year. Exports tend to be relatively low in the first quarter and relatively high in the second; while imports tend to be relatively high in the second and third quarters and relatively low in the fourth. Most of these variations are fairly small and so it is not surprising that the gross domestic product as a whole has a pattern rather similar to that of its biggest constituent, private consumers' expenditure.

CHAPTER V

COMPARISONS OVER SPACE

1. *Britain and America Compared: Levels*

IN Chapter IV we have seen how comparisons over time can be made in terms of a given set of relative values. We shall now see that exactly the same technique can be applied to comparisons over space. When we were considering index-number formulae in section 2 of the last chapter we identified the symbols 0 and 1 with two different periods. We might equally well have identified them with two different countries, and so built an index-number bridge across space instead of building it across time.

Let us take two countries, Britain and America. For each of them let us make a list of all the commodities which constitute final product. Now, assuming that Britain = 0 and America = 1, we can draw up a set of quantity ratios, q_1/q_0, which will show the quantity level of each commodity in America as a proportion of its quantity level in Britain. If we now multiply each of these ratios by the corresponding expenditure in Britain and add up the resulting values thus, $\Sigma[p_0q_0(q_1/q_0)]$, we shall have a measure of American final product valued at British prices. If we divide this by total expenditure in Britain, Σp_0q_0, we shall get Laspeyres' index-number of quantities, $\Sigma p_0q_1/\Sigma p_0q_0$, which compares the levels of final product in the two countries in terms of British relative prices. In a similar way we can calculate the corresponding Paasche quantity index, $\Sigma p_1q_1/\Sigma p_1q_0$, which compares them in terms of American prices.

Having determined the quantity indices, we can then obtain price indices by dividing the ratio of actual expenditure in the two countries, $\Sigma p_1 q_1/\Sigma p_0 q_0$, by either of the quantity indices. If we use Laspeyres' quantity index as the divisor we shall obtain Paasche's price index, $\Sigma p_1 q_1/\Sigma p_0 q_1$, which connects two valuations of American final product, one expressed in dollars, the other in pounds. If on the other hand we use Paasche's quantity index as the divisor we shall obtain Laspeyres' price index, $\Sigma p_1 q_0/\Sigma p_0 q_0$, which shows the relationship between the dollar and the pound valuations of British final product. By either operation we shall get a measure of the average purchasing power of the dollar in relation to the average purchasing power of the pound. As we have seen in the last chapter, however, the conclusions reached through Laspeyres' method may not tally with those reached through Paasche's, and in such cases the best answer devised so far is Fisher's ideal index, which is the geometric average of the other two.

On the whole, comparisons over space are more difficult to make and quantitatively less certain than comparisons over time, by which we mean reasonably short time-spans, say a generation. The reasons for this are: first, that relative values tend to differ more between countries than between two not very distant periods in the same country; second, that the individual commodities used to satisfy the same wants in different countries are often different and thus not easy to compare; and third, that the information available is also different in different countries, depending very much on the degree of development of the various statistical services and on the categories and classifications which they employ.

The most thorough analysis of comparative national products and price levels so far available is that by Gilbert and associates, published by the O.E.E.C in [23]. This study contains a detailed comparison between the United States and eight European countries, Britain, Belgium, Denmark, France, Germany, Italy, the Netherlands and Norway, in 1950 and 1955. America is treated as the base and each European country is compared with it first in terms of American relative prices and then in terms of its own prices. For certain purposes use is also made of a set of 'average European prices'. We shall see the point of this concept in section 3 below.

According to the Gilbert study, in 1950 the British gross national product *per head of the population* was 62 per cent of the American in terms of American relative prices but only 48 per cent in terms of British prices. The corresponding percentages for 1955 are 64 and 50. These quantity indices are respectively Laspeyres' and Paasche's with America treated as the base. The difference is considerable in both years, showing to what extent this kind of comparison is affected by the values chosen as weights, but we should not be disconcerted by it; after all, the two pairs of index-numbers do give us an idea of the range in which to place the British standard of living in respect to the American, and if we want to express its position by a single figure for each year we can take Fisher's index-numbers, which are 54 per cent in 1950 and 56 per cent in 1955.

The figures given in [23] refer to final product. There is however an alternative approach to international comparisons just as there is to comparisons over time, namely value added. This approach has been explored by Paige and Bombach in their comparison between Britain and America in [42]. While in principle the two approaches should lead to identical results, in this case the calculations done on value added were somewhat more favourable to Britain, suggesting that those done on final product overestimate the difference between the two countries.

But why, it may be asked, go to all this trouble to calculate the relative economic positions of Britain and America when we could simply compare totals through the official rate of exchange? The answer is that if we chose this apparently straightforward approach, the exchange rate, at that time approximately £1 = \$2·8, would place Britain at 37 per cent of the American level in 1950 and 42 per cent in 1955, which shows that despite the range of uncertainty of the index-number calculations the figures yielded by the exchange rate lie well outside that range and exaggerate the difference between the two countries. This confirms the common belief that after the devaluation of 1949 the internal purchasing power of the pound was officially undervalued in relation to that of the dollar. We shall see in the next section that in 1938 the position was reversed and it was the dollar that was undervalued in relation to the pound. The conclusion is that exchange rates, though temptingly simple, are a most unreliable guide and should as far as possible be avoided when making international comparisons.

2. *Britain and America Compared: Levels and Trends*

Tables 12 and 14 of the preceding chapter showed the course of the gross domestic product in Britain and America since 1938. In order to carry the comparison further back it is more convenient, however, to use national product totals. Annual estimates of the gross national product at constant prices are available in both countries well back into the nineteenth century; if we divide them year by year by the number of inhabitants and express the results in one currency we shall obtain two comparable series which will show the course of real product per head in each country. This is done for 1890–1970, using the pound as the currency unit, in table 17 below. The years of the two world wars are omitted in order to focus attention on more normal periods.

The two series in this table are linked together at one point, 1955, the course of each being determined by a comparison over time in each country. The exchange rate implied is £1 = \$3·4, which is the geometric average of the two price ratios yielded by Paasche's and Laspeyres' price indices for 1955.

As to the sources of the figures, the series for Britain after the second world war are based on the *Blue Book*. For earlier years they are based on the estimates of Feinstein shortly to be published in [19]; a provisional version of these estimates is available back to 1900 in [31] and we are grateful to Dr. Feinstein for allowing us to make use of his as yet unpublished

TABLE 17

Gross National Product per Head of the Population, 1890–1970 United Kingdom and United States

(1955 £)

	1890	1891	1892	1893	1894	1895	1896	1897	1898	1899	1900	1901	1902	1903
U.K.	213	218	213	210	219	224	232	230	241	251	244	251	251	249
U.S.	216	221	238	222	212	233	223	241	242	259	262	286	283	292
	1904	1905	1906	1907	1908	1909	1910	1911	1912	1913	1914 1919	1920	1921	1922
U.K.	248	249	255	253	244	250	256	261	260	272	..	237	223	230
U.S.	282	297	326	325	292	322	318	324	333	340	..	351	315	360
	1923	1924	1925	1926	1927	1928	1929	1930	1931	1932	1933	1934	1935	1936
U.K.	236	242	254	243	259	262	268	266	251	249	253	269	278	286
U.S.	396	388	414	432	426	423	447	398	365	308	301	326	356	402
	1937	1938	1939 1945	1946	1947	1948	1949	1950	1951	1952	1953	1954	1955	1956
U.K.	295	302	..	326	312	318	325	337	345	342	356	369	379	384
U.S.	421	397	..	591	575	590	580	626	664	673	691	670	708	709
	1957	1958	1959	1960	1961	1962	1963	1964	1965	1966	1967	1968	1969	1970
U.K.	390	390	402	418	429	430	444	465	474	480	487	500	507	515
U.S.	706	687	718	721	723	758	777	808	849	893	906	939	956	943

material. Throughout the period, the estimates of the gross domestic product are based on expenditure data; and the net income from abroad, which is the connecting link between the gross domestic and the gross national products, is reduced to constant prices by means of an index-number of import prices.

The whole series, which is expressed in terms of 1955 prices, is obtained by linking together subseries based on different systems of weights. The *Blue Book* figures back to 1963 are in terms of the relative prices of 1963 and the modifications of this weighting system implicit in the earlier postwar series were indicated on p. 104 above. The link between 1938 and 1948 is the geometric average of estimates made at 1938 and at 1948 prices. The interwar series is based on 1938 prices, as is also the link between 1913 and 1920. Up to 1913, the calculations are made at 1900 prices.

For 1920, calculations were made including and excluding Southern Ireland. On the basis of these figures a correction was made to the earlier estimates to allow for the fact that gross product per head in Southern Ireland is lower than in the rest of Britain. In principle, therefore, the whole series for Britain relates to Great Britain and Northern Ireland.

The series presented is the most uniform we have been able to construct, being based essentially on expenditure data throughout and relying entirely on the work of Feinstein up to 1938 and for the link between 1938 and 1948. It should be realized, however, that Feinstein has also produced series based on output and on income data; and furthermore, that Deane has recently produced a series of estimates for the years 1830 to 1913 [18]. Had we made use of these alternative series we should have obtained somewhat different results, particularly for the earlier years.

The figures for America are taken partly from the *Survey* and partly from Kendrick's estimates in [88]: the official series in the *Survey* has been used back to 1920 and to this have been linked for the years up to 1913 Kendrick's estimates based on 1929 relative values. The official series only extends back to 1909 and so could not have been used for our whole period. Over most of the 1920's and 1930's, the two series are very close together but for the few comparable years before the first world war the official series is somewhat higher than Kendrick's, and so it may be that we have underestimated the American position in the early years.

A final point that must be kept in mind is that the vertical distance between the two series is determined by the relationship of the £ to the $ as determined for 1955 in [23]. It would be comforting if we could check the relative levels of our series at another point, say 1900. Unfortunately we do not possess the data for such a study, and so we must await the results of future research to improve on the comparison we have made.

Table 17 makes it possible to compare the levels of product in Britain and America year by year but not to take in at a glance either their movements over time or their changing relationship to each other. All this becomes clear if the figures are represented graphically, as in diagram 3 below.

This diagram is provided with two units of measurement, 1955 pounds and 1955 dollars. As in the case of diagram 2, product levels are measured on a logarithmic scale, which means that an upward-sloping straight line corresponds to a constant proportionate rate of growth over time.

In studying diagram 3 the following comments may be useful. First, many factors make it difficult to summarize the growth of real product per head in either country in terms of simple trends. In the case of Britain, there are not only the setbacks due to the two world wars, absolute in the case of the first, relative to a trend projection from the inter-war years in the case of the second, but also the stagnant period in the first decade of the twentieth century. In the case of America, the whole inter-war period, with the exception of the years in the second half of the 1920's, lay well below the trend formed by connecting the period before 1913 with the period after 1946.

Second, if we try to account for these changing fortunes we might outline the forces at work in the following terms.

DIAGRAM 3

Gross National Product per Head of the Population, 1890–1970
United Kingdom and United States

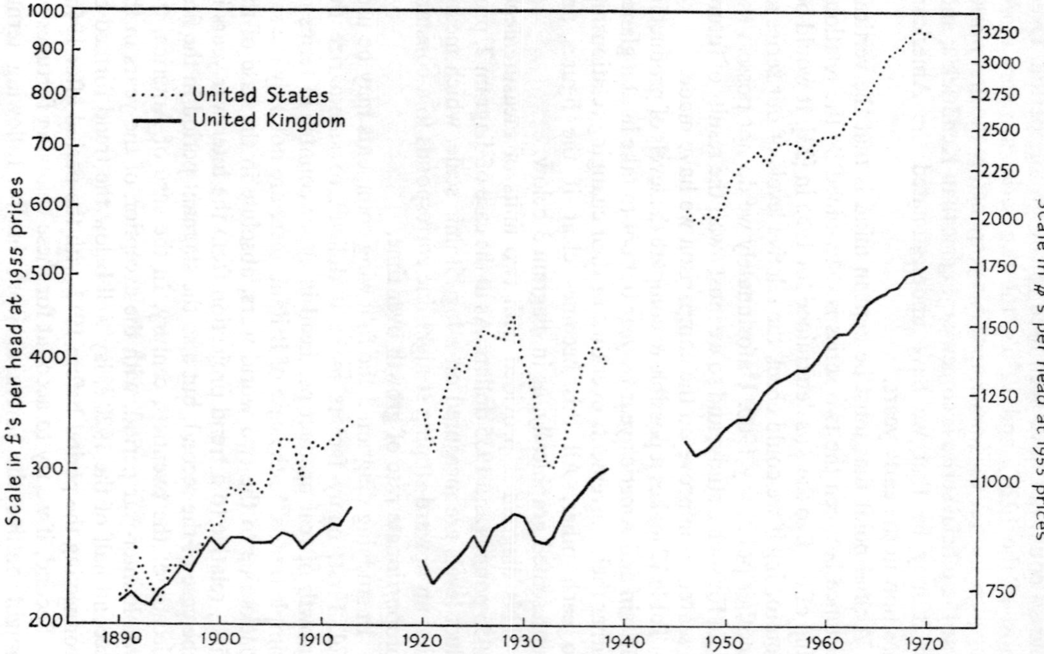

Abstracting from changes in the size of the population, which of course are not reflected in the per head figures of diagram 3, the main factor making for the growth of product is the capacity of a country for economic and technical innovation and adaptation. In this respect the two countries may not be so very different. The upward trends in Britain in the 1890's, the years immediately before the first world war, the inter-war period and the postwar period are not only similar to one another but are also similar to the trend of real product per head in America. To account for the extent to which the performance of the two economies has pulled apart, there would appear to be two major influences. The first might be described as a breakdown of social cohesion, evident in Britain in the early 1900's and in America, to a much greater extent than in Britain, in the 1930's. The second influence is the impact of major wars which, normally, may be expected to be adverse, as exemplified by the setback to Britain which followed the first world war. But this does not always happen; the second world war lifted the American economy out of the morass of the 1930's and, wiser counsels prevailing after the war than before it, the American economy did not slip back into instability, though it has not been as stable as the British economy in the last twenty-five years.

Third, when we compare the two countries we see that, from being very close together in the 1890's, the American series has gradually crept ahead but in a somewhat uneven manner. America did not stagnate in the early 1900's, as did Britain, and so by 1913 its product per head was about 25 per cent higher than Britain's; by 1924 the difference had increased to 60 per cent, only to fall to 19 per cent in 1933; in 1938 it had increased again to 31 per cent. The second world war, by turning America into an arsenal, absorbed all the labour unemployed in the 1930's and gave an abnormal stimulus to production, with the result that in 1946 the difference between the two countries increased to 81 per cent. With fluctuations between 69 per cent in 1961 and 89 per cent in 1969, the difference returned to 83 per cent in 1970, almost the same figure as in 1946. The difference for 1969 may be compared with the crude calculation made on p. 26 above.

Fourth, as we have already seen, the further back one goes the harder it is to determine levels with accuracy and the more controversial the estimates become. Thus, again taking Britain, the fall of about 7 per cent shown by our figures between 1911 and 1924, the two best-documented years on either side of the first war, may seem exaggerated unless one remembers: (i) that the gross national product does not relate to domestic production alone but is the sum of the gross domestic product and of net income from abroad, and that the latter fell substantially, in real terms, after the war; and (ii) that the gross national product measures the output of national resources and therefore excludes imports, so that the improvement which took place for Britain in the terms of trade after the war, whereby Britain could buy relatively cheap and sell relatively dear and thus consume and accumulate more per unit of output in 1924 than in 1911, has no weight in this comparison. Indeed Bowley and Stamp, comparing the same two years in [7], published in 1927, reached much the same conclusion as we do. Like us, these authors based their calculations on money values and price movements and it is interesting to note that to them, far from appearing pessimistic, a fall of 5 per cent between 1911 and 1924 appeared surprisingly small when compared with the production statistics then available; we know now, from the later researches of Lomax [30] and others, that these statistics considerably underestimated the rise in production during the first quarter of the century.

Finally, it is interesting to compare the price ratios of the two countries with the course of the exchange rate between the dollar and the pound. This is done for selected years in table 18 below.

The falling series in the first column of this table shows simply that prices have been rising faster in Britain than in America, with the consequence that through time the pound has

TABLE 18

Dollar-Pound Equivalents, 1913–1969

	Price ratios linked in 1955	Exchange rates
1913 ..	5·3	4·9
1924 ..	4·6	4·4
1938 ..	4·1	4·9
1950 ..	3·8	2·8
1955 ..	3·4	2·8
1960 ..	3·3	2·8
1965 ..	3·0	2·8
1969 ..	2·9	2·4

come to buy less and less in comparison with the dollar. The series in the second column shows the course of the exchange rate. In spite of the fact that the two series move in the same general direction, a glance at the figures brings out once again the danger of using exchange rates for the purpose of international comparisons. This is recognized when exchange rates are fixed officially but may apply quite as strongly when they are not. Even under free market conditions it is not to be expected that they will exactly reflect the ratio of internal prices: there may be political reasons why a particular currency is either specially sought after or mistrusted abroad, or the products exported by a country may be highly specialized, so that the national price level will be unrepresentative of their price level on the international market. Thus we see that the pound from being undervalued in 1913 got even in 1924 and became considerably overvalued between 1924 and 1938, owing partly to the political unrest of continental Europe and partly perhaps to the American depression; the position was reversed in the devaluation of 1949, thereby giving Britain some export advantage over America; but the persistently higher rate of increase in British prices has much reduced this advantage and is bringing the two series together again. If we had compared Britain and America in 1924 on the basis of the exchange rate we should not have gone seriously wrong, but in 1938 we should have overestimated the British national product by about one fifth, and underestimated it by about one fifth in 1955.

It is important not to claim too much for the kind of comparison made in this section: we have seen something of the theoretical difficulties involved and these are increased by the incompleteness of the available statistics, especially for the more distant past. But it is even more important not to adopt a nihilistic attitude to such comparisons; if carefully done, they provide the best guide we have to relative levels and trends and are the most reliable means of judging economic performance and acheivement in different parts of the world.

3. *Rings and Chains of Comparisons*

Before we go on to the other European countries included in the Gilbert study [23], let us digress for a moment on the comparison of three or more situations, whether in space or in time. Suppose we have three countries, or three periods, distinguished by the suffixes 0, 1 and 2. If we compared first 0 with 1, then 1 with 2 and finally 2 with 0 we might hope to end up with the same value for 0 that we started from; in other words, the product of the binary comparisons round the ring should multiply out to 1. We can be certain that this result will follow identically only if the same set of relative values is used for all the comparisons, though in freak cases it may follow by chance even if this condition is not satisfied.

This statement can be verified by extending the formulae given in section 2 of Chapter IV above. If we go round the ring of comparisons using Laspeyres' quantity index for each link we obtain

$$\frac{\Sigma p_0 q_1}{\Sigma p_0 q_0} \cdot \frac{\Sigma p_1 q_2}{\Sigma p_1 q_1} \cdot \frac{\Sigma p_2 q_0}{\Sigma p_2 q_2} \neq 1 \qquad \ldots (9)$$

because, in general, the terms of the product do not cancel out.

Thus the ring is not properly closed. If we now try using Fisher's ideal index-number we obtain

$$\sqrt{\frac{\Sigma p_0 q_1}{\Sigma p_0 q_0} \cdot \frac{\Sigma p_1 q_1}{\Sigma p_1 q_0}} \cdot \sqrt{\frac{\Sigma p_1 q_2}{\Sigma p_1 q_1} \cdot \frac{\Sigma p_2 q_2}{\Sigma p_2 q_1}} \cdot \sqrt{\frac{\Sigma p_2 q_0}{\Sigma p_2 q_2} \cdot \frac{\Sigma p_0 q_0}{\Sigma p_0 q_2}}$$

$$= \sqrt{\frac{\Sigma p_0 q_1}{\Sigma p_0 q_2} \cdot \frac{\Sigma p_1 q_2}{\Sigma p_1 q_0} \cdot \frac{\Sigma p_2 q_0}{\Sigma p_2 q_1}} \neq 1 \qquad \ldots (10)$$

in general, and again the ring is not closed. It will be noticed that in this case each of the three binary comparisons is based on the values of the third country. If more than three countries are compared, the ideal index-number ring, after the cancellation of common terms, has an appearance even more surprising than (10).

The position is different if we choose a common set of relative values for all the comparisons. Let p_c denote prices, c being the country whose values we choose. Then clearly

$$\frac{\Sigma p_c q_1}{\Sigma p_c q_0} \cdot \frac{\Sigma p_c q_2}{\Sigma p_c q_1} \cdot \frac{\Sigma p_c q_0}{\Sigma p_c q_2} = 1 \qquad \ldots (11)$$

identically, since each of the three distinct terms appears in both the numerator and the denominator of this expression. From the point of view of consistency it does not matter what set of relative values is used provided it is the same in each comparison: c may equal 0, 1, 2 or a fourth country outside the comparison, or an average of all or any of these. From the point of view of relevance, however, we must be careful of how we choose c, since if we choose a country whose relative values are very different from those of the countries under comparison we may get a misleading answer.

We can now see the point of the concept of average European prices mentioned in section 1 above. Each direct comparison of a European country with America gives us the best comparison we can make of that country with America, but for intra-European comparisons there is no reason why we should bring American values into the picture; nor is there any reason why we should select the values of any one European country in preference to those of any other. By establishing a set of average European values we get round the difficulty and can compare the eight European countries covered in [23] on a basis which though not ideal will be consistent and fairly relevant. This is done in the form of a ready reckoner in table 19 below. The percentages refer to real product per head.

TABLE 19

Relative Gross National Products per Head in 1955

(*1955 average European prices*)

	United Kingdom	Norway	Belgium	Denmark	Germany	France	Nether-lands	Italy
United Kingdom	1·00	1·02	1·04	1·11	1·15	1·17	1·22	2·12
Norway	0·98	1·00	1·03	1·09	1·13	1·15	1·20	2·09
Belgium	0·96	0·98	1·00	1·06	1·10	1·12	1·17	2·03
Denmark	0·90	0·92	0·94	1·00	1·04	1·06	1·10	1·91
Germany	0·87	0·88	0·91	0·96	1·00	1·02	1·06	1·84
France	0·85	0·87	0·89	0·95	0·98	1·00	1·04	1·81
Netherlands	0·82	0·83	0·86	0·91	0·94	0·96	1·00	1·74
Italy	0·47	0·48	0·49	0·52	0·54	0·55	0·57	1·00

Reading this table horizontally, each row gives the country named at its side as a percentage of the countries named at the head of the columns; thus the row for Denmark shows that in 1955 the Danish gross national product per head was 90 per cent of the British and 106 per cent of the French. Reading the table vertically, each column gives all the countries listed down the side as percentages of that named at its head; thus the column for Denmark shows that the British and the French national products were respectively 111 per cent and 95 per cent of the Danish. The consistency of the comparisons is easily checked; for example, if we form the product of the comparisons of France with Britain, Denmark with France, the Netherlands with Denmark, and Italy with the Netherlands we shall reach, apart from rounding-off errors, the same figure as appears in the direct comparison of Italy with Britain: $0{\cdot}85 \times 1{\cdot}06 \times 0{\cdot}91 \times 0{\cdot}57 = 0{\cdot}47$.

If, however, we want to obtain a consistent comparison and at the same time follow as closely as possible the individual price and quantity structures of each of the countries concerned, then we must adopt a more sophisticated method than that used in [23]. Such a method has been developed and illustrated by van Ijzeren in [27] and a simple form of solution has been suggested by Geary in [21].

The figures in table 19 are now somewhat out of date and we might ask how far they reflect the present ranking of the countries. To answer the question properly we should need another comparative study like [23] and fortunately one is under way, though we cannot expect the results in the immediate future. In the meantime we can make an approximate calculation as follows. The O.E.C.D. regularly compiles the national accounts of member countries on a comparable basis, and in [39] brings together information for the years 1950 through 1968. One of the series relates to gross national product per head at constant prices; in the case of Britain this series rose by 33 per cent between 1955 and 1968, in the case of Norway it rose by 54 per cent, and so on. If we follow the ordering of countries given in table 19, we can use the time series to measure the movement in each country from 1955 to 1968 and standardize the 1968 figures with, again, the gross national product per head in Britain equal to one. In this way we obtain, in place of the first column of table 19, the numbers $\{1{\cdot}00\ 1{\cdot}14\ 1{\cdot}06\ 1{\cdot}09\ 1{\cdot}09\ 1{\cdot}07\ 0{\cdot}93\ 0{\cdot}65\}$. By comparing the two sets of figures we can see that in the thirteen years from 1955 to 1968 each of the other countries had improved its position relatively to Britain, and that Britain, instead of being top of the list, had been overtaken by Norway, Belgium, Denmark, Germany and France.

Can we check these calculations, or at least find out whether they exaggerate the worsening of Britain's position vis-à-vis her neighbours in Western Europe? Until the new comparative study is published the answer is effectively no, since the alternative is to use exchange rates, which we have seen to be unreliable for the purpose of inter-country comparisons. However, for another purpose, namely to construct indicators for a number of countries grouped into a single economic region, exchange rates can be reasonably used as weights when aggregating the series for the component countries. This is done by the O.E.C.D. in [38], which shows both the aggregated indicators and their component series, all expressed in dollars. On this basis, the position of Britain appears even less favourable than our approximate comparison suggests.

4. *Europe and America Compared: the Composition of Gross National Product*

In this section we shall compare final product in America with final product in Europe as represented by all the member countries of the O.E.E.C. In [23] each of the eight countries so far considered is compared with America both on the basis of American prices and on that of average European prices, and to complete the picture rough estimates are also given for the remaining member countries, namely Austria, Greece, Iceland, Ireland, Luxembourg, Portugal, Sweden, Switzerland and Turkey, as a group. The results of these comparisons are then summarized in a set of geometric averages which are reproduced in table 20 below. The unit of currency used is the dollar. The definitions of the main components of final product are similar to those used throughout this book but there are certain differences; of these the most important is that all expenditure on health and education is included in private consumption, so that government consumption is restricted to general administration and defence.

Quite a lot can be learnt from this table. In the first place, by studying the figures as they are we can get an idea of the productiveness of the different countries and of the size of the market for each category of product. For instance, if we compare the first two columns we see that in 1955 the O.E.E.C. countries as a whole produced 27 per cent less than America

TABLE 20

Comparative Gross National Products by Major Categories in 1955

(*Money values in $ milliard; population in million*)

	United States	O.E.E.C. member countries	8 countries combined	United Kingdom	Norway	Belgium	Denmark	Germany	France	Netherlands	Italy	Other O.E.E.C member countries
1. Gross national product*	377·2	274·1	235·5	66·3	4·3	10·8	5·1	57·6	48·6	11·4	31·5	38·6
2. Private consumption (including health and education)	250·3	185·0	157·7	45·9	2·8	6·9	3·6	36·7	33·8	7·0	21·0	27·3
(*a*) Food	62·7	68·8	57·8	14·6	0·9	2·5	1·2	14·3	12·3	2·8	9·3	11·0
(*b*) Clothing	26·1	18·0	15·2	4·3	0·4	0·9	0·4	3·4	3·1	0·8	2·0	2·9
(*c*) Housing	16·0	13·2	11·3	4·0	0·2	0·4	0·3	2·6	2·2	0·5	1·1	1·9
(*d*) Consumers' durables	32·7	8·9	7·5	2·5	0·1	0·2	0·2	2·6	1·5	0·2	0·3	1·3
(*e*) Other goods and services ..	112·7	76·2	65·9	20·5	1·3	2·9	1·5	13·9	14·8	2·7	8·3	10·2
3. Government consumption ..	51·3	34·7	30·0	9·5	0·4	1·2	0·5	6·4	5·8	1·6	4·5	4·7
(*a*) General administration ..	11·1	18·6	15·3	3·5	0·2	0·7	0·3	4·0	3·0	0·8	2·9	3·3
(*b*) Defence	40·2	16·2	14·7	6·0	0·2	0·6	0·2	2·4	2·9	0·8	1·6	1·5
4. Domestic investment	74·4	53·0	45·9	10·7	1·1	2·5	0·9	13·7	8·3	2·5	6·2	7·1
(*a*) Producers' durables	30·1	21·4	19·2	5·1	0·4	1·4	0·5	5·2	3·7	1·2	1·8	2·3
(*b*) Construction	38·2	27·8	23·3	4·7	0·7	0·9	0·4	7·1	4·2	1·1	4·1	4·5
(i) residential	12·8	15·5	13·4	2·9	0·3	0·6	0·2	5·3	2·1	0·4	1·6	2·1
(ii) other	25·4	12·3	9·9	1·8	0·4	0·4	0·2	1·8	2·2	0·7	2·5	2·4
(*c*) Increase in stocks	6·1	3·8	3·5	0·9	0·0	0·2	0·0	1·4	0·4	0·2	0·4	0·3
5. Net exports	1·2	1·4	1·9	0·1	–0·1	0·3	0·0	0·9	0·7	0·2	–0·2	–0·5
6. Population	164·5	284·1	219·4	51·0	3·4	8·9	4·4	49·9	43·3	10·7	47·8	64·7

* Components do not always add up to totals because of rounding-off errors.

did, although their combined population exceeded that of America by 73 per cent, and that despite their much greater number the Europeans consumed very little more food than was consumed in America and spent on durables only about one-quarter of what the Americans did.

In the second place, by dividing the items in each column by the respective population figures (row 6) we can assess the actual money value of product and expenditure per head in the different countries and form a fairly concrete estimate of the different standards of living. For instance, total production per head was $2,293 in America, $1,300 in Britain, $1,154 in Germany and $659 in Italy; the amount of dollars per head spent on food in these same countries was respectively 382, 286, 287 and 195; that spent on consumers' durables, 198, 49, 52 and 6; that spent on fixed investment, 415, 192, 246 and 121; and that spent on public administration alone, 68, 69, 80 and 61. This last, exceptionally constant, series is a striking confirmation of the view that public administration is an overhead which varies directly with the number of inhabitants, irrespective of their average income.

In the third place, by dividing the items in each column by their sum (row 1) we can find out in what proportion each component of product contributes to the total. Taking the main categories first, we see that, on average, private consumption accounts for about two-thirds of final product, public consumption for about one-seventh and fixed investment for about one-sixth, the remainder being made up of investment in stocks and net exports, both comparatively unimportant quantities. From country to country there are considerable variations from these averages, however, but they seem to be a matter of national idiosyncrasies, quite unconnected with either size or standard of living. For instance, in America and Italy, which are at the opposite ends of the income scale, the proportion of product devoted to private consumption was the same, between 66 and 67 per cent, while in Denmark and the Netherlands, which are both in the middle range, it was 71 and 61 per cent respectively. The percentage devoted to public consumption ranged from 14 in America, Britain, the Netherlands and Italy to 10 in Denmark and only 9 in Norway. Fixed investment shows the same unpredictable pattern: in Britain the percentage was as low as 15, in Norway, with almost the same product per head, it was as high as 26.

We can get a more enlightening picture of the spending patterns of the different countries if we subdivide the main percentages into their subcomponents. All sorts of combinations and permutations are possible and the reader should have no difficulty in constructing his own tables of percentages in any way he thinks interesting. A summary which throws some light on the relationship between spending patterns and income levels is given in table 21 below as an example, with the European countries collected together in two groups: the first,

TABLE 21

The Allocation of Gross National Product in Relation to Product per Head in 1955

	United States	Northern and Western Europe	Southern Europe
1. Percentages of gross national product*			
(*a*) Private consumption	66	67	69
(i) Food	17	24	29
(ii) Clothing	7	6	7
(iii) Housing	4	5	4
(iv) Consumers' durables	9	4	2
(v) Other goods and services	30	28	26
(*b*) Government consumption	14	12	13
(i) General administration	3	6	9
(ii) Defence	11	6	4
(*c*) Domestic investment in fixed assets ..	18	18	18
(i) Producers' durables	8	9	6
(ii) Construction	10	9	12
(*d*) Increase in stocks and net exports	2	3	0
2. Gross national product per head (*in 1955* $)..	2,293	1,189	623

* Percentages do not always add up to totals because of rounding-off errors.

called Northern and Western Europe, contains the richest seven of the eight; the second, called Southern Europe, is made up of Italy and the 'other' O.E.E.C. countries.

Bearing in mind that rich regions have more of all the main categories of goods and services than poor regions have, the conclusions to be drawn from this table are: (i) the richer the country the smaller the proportion of income spent on food and the larger the proportions spent on durables and other goods and services, while those spent on clothing and housing stay constant; (ii) the poorer the country the larger the proportion of its resources absorbed by public administration and the smaller, as a general rule, that absorbed by defence; and (iii) though in fixed investment the pattern is not so definite, it appears that the richer countries invest relatively more in producers' durables and relatively less in construction than do the poorer countries.

CHAPTER VI

WHERE DO WE GO FROM HERE?

1. *Summary*

IN THE preceding chapters we have described the main conceptual problems which arise in accounting for the transactions in an economic system. We have shown how the main totals of income and product are related to one another and how they are built up from their constituents. We have examined the various ways in which income is redistributed among sectors and, within the personal sector, the incidence of taxes and social service benefits on different kinds of household. We have discussed the question of comparing product totals over time and space and have explained how in making comparisons we must distinguish between figures expressed in the currency units of a particular place and time and those expressed in a common unit of purchasing power.

By these means we have introduced step by step the basic information needed to describe and compare economic systems in quantitative terms. This information has been organized within an accounting framework designed to distinguish between the activities of production, consumption and accumulation and between the domestic economy and the rest of the world. Before finally closing down we shall indicate briefly how by extending this framework we can increase the scope of our analysis and unite the main branches of economic and social statistics into a much broader but equally coherent system.

2. *The United Nations' System*

During the second half of the 1960's the United Nations' old system of national accounts [75] was substantially revised and a new version was published at the end of 1968 [76]. The main object of this revision was to extend the earlier version to include a detailed treatment of economic connections, particularly in the fields of production and finance. The point of departure in this extension is a simple set of four accounts of the nation, essentially the same as that given in Chapter II above, which is gradually disaggregated to provide additional detail and expanded to include information on stocks (balance-sheet data) as well as on flows. The structure of the system is illustrated by a matrix with eighty-eight balancing rows and columns, which correspond to the main subdivisions of the system. The content of these rows and columns is then elaborated and set out in the form of standard accounts and tables.

This *System of National Accounts*, usually abbreviated to *S.N.A.*, is followed by many countries. Russia and other communist countries, however, make use of a somewhat different set of concepts, the sytem of material product balances, usually abbreviated to M.P.S. A statement of the basic methodology of the M.P.S. was presented to the Statistical Commission of the United Nations at its sixteenth session [78]. In recent years the links between the two systems have been intensively studied at the Economic Commission for Europe in Geneva. A simplified comparative statement, based on the numerical example in [76], is given in [50, pp. 201–23]. A description, in matrix terms, of the Hungarian variant of the M.P.S. is given by Árvay in [2].

3. *Input-Output*

When we were examining the domestic product account in section 3 of Chapter II above we imagined this account to have been constructed by consolidating all the production accounts in the economy. As a consequence we lost all the flows of intermediate product. If we want to study the productive system in detail we must retrieve this information, since in most industries a considerable part of the costs of production consists of purchases from other industries and in many industries a considerable part of the revenue from production comes from sales to other industries. We can do this by subdividing the production account so that we have one account for each branch of production. If we arrange these accounts in a system of rows and columns so that the elements in a given row relate to the revenues (outputs) of a particular industry and the elements in the corresponding column relate to the costs (inputs) of the same industry, we obtain the familiar form of input-output table. In addition to the industry rows and columns, this table will contain an extra row and column whose elements will be respectively the primary inputs into the different branches of production and the final outputs emerging from them.

The construction of input-output tables was pioneered over a generation ago by Leontief and applied by him to the American economy in [28,29]. The rapid growth of the subject can be traced in the proceedings of a series of international conferences on input-output techniques [4, 5, 10, 35]. A brief description of the way in which an input-output table fits into the social accounts is given in [55]; a fuller treatment of taxonomic questions will be found in [46]; and an excellent survey of inter-industry economics by Chenery and Clark appears in [15]. The subject is treated in considerable detail in [76].

For Britain, official tables for 1954 and 1963 are given in [57, 67]; and *Economic Trends* for January 1971 gives provisional tables for 1968. Projected tables are constructed from time to time by the group working on the Cambridge Growth Project, examples for 1972 being given in [8]. Apart from the small tables which appear occasionally in the *Blue Book*, several tables have been constructed for earlier years, notably 1948 [44], 1935 [3] and even 1907 [16, pp. 183–220]. Many input-output tables have been constructed for America; the latest official one relates to 1958 and was published in the *Survey* for September 1965.

4. *Income Distributions*

We have already touched on this subject in section 4 of Chapter III above, in connection with the redistributive effects of taxes and social service benefits. As we have seen, a great deal of information about the distribution of incomes by size and by family characteristics is published regularly in [72]. Tax returns provide another important source, and up to 1969 information on the distribution of personal income before and after tax was given for selected calendar years in the *Blue Book*. Since 1970 this table has been dropped because of the increasing amount of estimation required to produce calendar-year figures on a national accounts basis. Tables for financial years, obtained by the Inland Revenue from income surveys of tax returns, are published in [59, 71]. Further sources are private surveys, like the Oxford Savings Survey as described for example by Lydall in [32], and studies relating to specific professions or occupations such as medical practitioners or farm workers. Information on the distribution of incomes in America can be found in the *Survey*, in [83, pp. 40–6] and in [85].

If we consider a group of individuals following a single occupation, we might reasonably suppose the distribution of their incomes to be governed by some comparatively simple law and so to approximate to a simple form. If we assume this law to be Gibrat's law of proportional effect [22], we should expect to observe a lognormal distribution of incomes. In [1] Aitchison and Brown give a number of examples to show that this is in fact the case; but they also show that the law governing the distribution of incomes in general cannot be simple and that systematic departures are found from lognormality. In [13] and [14, vol. 2, ch. 18] Champernowne analyses the generation of income as a Markov process and shows the conditions under which an equilibrium lognormal distribution will emerge.

5. *Flows of Funds*

When we come to capital transactions we again find that on subdividing the national accounts by sectors we obtain a large number of flows which are lost when the sector accounts are consolidated. Thus in the consolidated accounts of Chapter II there is no trace of the *flows of funds* whereby one sector puts its saving, either by means of loans or by means of capital transfers, at the disposal of another. This information begins to emerge only in Chapter III, when a certain degree of deconsolidation is introduced. If we wish to study monetary phenomena in detail, however, we must carry the process of deconsolidation further; we must bring into play a type of sector which is hardly noticeable when studying production and consumption, namely the financial sector, since financial intermediaries such as banks, insurance companies, building societies and the like play an important role in the direction of funds, although their role in production and consumption is of secondary importance.

Until fairly recently not much research had been done in Britain on this subject, but since the publication of the Radcliffe Report on the working of the monetary system [68], British financial statistics have been very considerably improved. From 1964 onwards a substantial amount of information on flows of funds has been published in [56] and in the *Blue Book*; these estimates are discussed by Berman in [6]. More recently still, as part of the work of the Cambridge Growth Project, Roe [9] has set up for the years 1962–66 detailed flow-of-funds accounts in which as many as thirty-four sectors are distinguished and the transactions relate to eight types of tangible asset and forty-three types of financial claim.

For America, an accounting system intended to emphasize this aspect of economic transactions was first devised by Copeland in [17] as a study of 'moneyflows' and has been developed by the Federal Reserve System in [80]. Up-to-date information appears from time to time in [79].

6. *National and Sector Balance Sheets*

All the concepts which have been described so far relate to *flows*, that is, so much produced, consumed, due to be paid, due to be received, transferred, lent, borrowed, etc., *per unit of time*. To obtain a complete accounting system we must also account for *stocks*, not in the limited sense of products awaiting sale or use but in the more general sense of *assets* and *liabilities* existing *at a point in time*; that is to say, we must set up a national *balance sheet*. In a world in which values were constant this balance sheet might be presented in a form similar to the account for capital transactions, except that in front of each item we should have to put the word 'accumulated' to show that the figures referred to the total stock accumulated over the past and not to the latest addition to that stock represented by the flow for the current period; we should also omit the accumulated depreciation from the liabilities and subtract it from the accumulated fixed investment which forms the major component of assets. A table thus drawn up would show on the assets side the wealth of the economy as composed of: (i) the depreciated (written-down) value of all fixed assets; (ii) the value of stocks in the narrow sense of raw materials not yet used up, goods for sale and work in progress; and (iii) net claims outstanding against the rest of the world. On the liabilities side, the table would show the capital financing this wealth as composed of: (i) the accumulated saving of the economy; and (ii) the accumulated capital transfers (net) from the rest of the world. In practice, values do not remain constant and so it is necessary to account for the revaluations of assets and liabilities from one year's end to the next, as well as for the transactions (flows of funds) of the intervening period.

The construction of national balance sheets is related to the older studies of the national capital in the same way as the construction of national accounts is related to the older studies of the national income. Except in America, work on stocks has tended to lag behind work on flows but the position is changing; national and sector balance sheets now form an integral part of the *S.N.A.*, though the details have not yet been spelt out in full.

For Britain, a detailed series of national and sector balance sheets for the years 1957–61 was first constructed by Revell in [43]. In [9] Roe has brought the series up to 1966, complementing the balance sheets for the last five years with their related flow-of-funds and revaluation accounts. A useful summary of the results for the whole ten-year period was published by these two authors in the May 1971 issue of *Economic Trends*. From this it can be seen that between 1957 and 1966 the national wealth of Britain increased in money terms from about £60 milliard to about £140 milliard, or from about £1,150 to about £2,500 per head of the population.

For America, the outstanding work on this subject has been carried out by Goldsmith and his colleagues and has been published in a series of books and papers such as [24, 25].

7. *Subdividing the Balance of Payments*

The account for the rest of the world in table 6 above was made up of all the loose ends from the three accounts for production, consumption and accumulation, and thus closed the system. The entries in this account were arranged in a particular way which was convenient for the purpose in hand. They could, however, be elaborated and rearranged to provide a detailed statement of incomings and outgoings between Britain and the rest of the world. Even so, in many cases a simple account treating the rest of the world as if it were a single entity is not enough; it is necessary to have an articulated set of accounts in which each type of transaction that the country has with the outside world is subdivided and appropriately distributed among different economic groupings.

Detailed information on the British balance of payments, with some subdivision of the rest of the world into economic groupings such as Western Europe and the overseas sterling area, is given in [63]. Earlier estimates for the years 1946–57 were published in [74].

Similar information for America is to be found in [86].

8. *Regional Accounts*

The remarks of the preceding section on the advantages of geographical subdivision are applicable not only to the rest of the world. Throughout this book we have treated the national economy as a single, simple system but there is no reason why it should not be thought of as a complex system composed of several sub-systems, the country's regions, each with its own set of accounts drawn up on the same lines as the accounts of the nation. As might be expected, however, this extension of the concept of national accounting brings with it difficulties of its own. At the theoretical level there is, for instance, the question of how to handle supra-regional institutions like the central government. At the practical level there is the problem of collecting information on inter-regional flows of goods, to say nothing of inter-regional transfers and financial flows. A general survey of methods of regional description and analysis is given in [47], together with a bibliography of the subject up to 1960.

As to actual data, enough have already been collected both in Britain and in America to enable many of the entries in the national accounts to be subdivided by region. A tentative set of accounts for the twelve standard regions of Britain in 1948, based on the unpublished work of Miss Phyllis Deane, can be found in [47]. A more firmly based set of estimates relating to the early 1960's is given by Woodward in [89]. The reports of the Economic Planning Councils, as exemplified by [69], contain a large though varying amount of information for each region, and partial data for all twelve regions, relating for instance to personal expenditure and earnings from employment, are given in [58]. Finally, some information is available for Scotland in [33], Wales in [36, 37] and Northern Ireland in [11, 12, 70].

For America, data on state income payments are given in [87] and in the *Survey*. Income estimates have also been made for smaller regions, there are numerous regional input-output tables and a considerable literature exists on the economic analysis of regions in general.

9. *Social Accounting, Economic and Demographic*

The term *social accounting* was introduced into economics by Hicks in the preface to [26], which first appeared in 1942. It means, in the words of its originator, 'nothing else but the accounting of the whole community or nation, just as private accounting is the accounting of the individual firm'. In other words, it denotes the economic accounts of society. We entitled Chapter II 'From national income to national accounts', implying the transition from a *single magnitude*, the basic total of income, to a *structure* in which this magnitude is related to others of a similar kind. The transition from national accounts to social accounts as Hicks defines them involves perhaps a smaller step conceptually, the replacement of a relatively simple structure by a more elaborate one rather than the replacement of a magnitude by a structure, but a much bigger step from a practical point of view, because the amount of additional data required for the second transition is very large and its integration into a coherent system presents formidable difficulties. These developments form the subject matter of the new *S.N.A.*

But there is another field of enquiry which deserves to be included in an enlarged concept of the social accounts: for many purposes it would be useful to account for stocks and flows of human beings and to link these demographic and social data to the information given in the economic accounts. This is now widely recognized by economists as well as by sociologists and demographers.

The demographic aspect of social accounting starts by tracing the connections between the opening and closing stocks of a population. The opening stock consists of all the individuals present in the country at the beginning of, say, a year. Suppose we were to subdivide this opening stock into a number of categories, or *states*, defined by age-group and principal activity. Of the individuals found in each state at the beginning of the year, some would die in the course of the year, some would emigrate and the remainder would survive in the country to the end of the year. Of these survivors, some would remain in their initial state, others would change to other states: some schoolboys would go to university, some undergraduates would take jobs, some employees would retire, and so on. At the same time, there would be an inflow of new entrants brought about by births and immigrations. The closing stock consists of the survivors *plus* the new entrants, all classified by their terminal state. In this way we can account for the numbers in each category of the opening and closing stocks, showing respectively where they go to and where they come from.

So far we have been concerned only with identities: the individuals in each state of the opening stock either survive and remain in the country or leave it through death or emigration; and the individuals in each state of the closing stock are either survivors or new entrants. We can get a stage further if we assume that the individuals in any given state at the beginning of the year have fixed probabilities of remaining in that state throughout the year or moving to any one of the other states. On this assumption, the composition of the closing stock can be calculated from the opening stock and the new entrants of the year. In form, the relationships are similar to those of an open input-output model in economics; but whereas in economics the relationships connect total output to final output, in the present case they connect total population to new entrants.

We can get a stage further still by remembering that total cost, or price, can be built up from the costs of the constituent inputs. For example, a year spent in each learning activity involves a certain educational cost. If we know the cost of each learning activity, we can work out not only the costs incurred in this year's education but also the total cost that will be incurred, on average, in completing the education of an individual now in any state, educational or otherwise. A small child has the whole of his education in the future; an employee may have a certain probability of returning for a time to being a student and so will incur, on average, certain educational costs in the future although his regular education has been completed.

By such means we can link together economic accounting and the accounting for human stocks and flows in social demography. Various aspects of this subject are discussed in [48 to 54].

10. *Facts, Theories and Analysis*

In conclusion we shall try to trace the connections between social accounting on the one hand and theory and analysis on the other. In what follows we shall confine ourselves to economics, though what we have to say is equally applicable to social demography.

The economic aspect of social accounting is concerned with a comprehensive, orderly, consistent presentation of the facts of economic life, in which the concepts, definitions and classifications adopted lend themselves to actual measurement and, within this limitation, correspond to those which appear in economic theory and so can be used for economic analysis. Thus even if we start from an empirical point of view we shall find ourselves listening to the suggestions of theory at every turn: it is not the facts themselves that lead us to distinguish between current and capital expenditure, we do so at the suggestion of theory despite the difficulties involved in carrying out the distinction; nor is it the facts themselves that lead us to emphasize the national income as the basic total both of a country's income and of its contribution to world production. And so it is all the way through. The facts we present and the way we arrange them depend a great deal on considerations of theory.

The same is true if we start from a theoretical point of view. We may begin with purely theoretical concepts, like utility, which we have not yet learnt how to measure, but somewhere along the line our theories must connect with concepts to which we can give an empirical content, and so enable us to state expectations about the real world. For if this link is missing, we can hold any theory we wish, provided it is logically consistent, but we cannot speak of such a theory as being true or false since it says nothing about the real world and consequently cannot be supported or refuted by an appeal to facts. In other words, for a theory to be meaningful it must have empirical consequences and for it to be useful these consequences must relate to observable phenomena. Thus, useful theories cannot be developed independently of what can be observed any more than useful facts can be established without some regard to theoretical considerations.

Facts and theories meet in analysis. The combination of the two is essential if economics is to progress, since it is neither a pure subject, like mathematics, of which one does not ask that the theories should be applicable to actual phenomena, nor is it a collection of facts, like the objects on a junk heap, of which one does not ask how they are related. For 'balanced growth' in economics it is necessary to keep the facts and theories in line so that they can be related to one another. To help with this work is the main object of this book.

A LIST OF WORKS CITED

1. AITCHISON, J., and J. A. C. BROWN. *The Lognormal Distribution*. Cambridge University Press, 1957.
2. ÁRVAY, János. Development of the national accounting system in Hungary. *The Review of Income and Wealth*, series 15, no. 2, 1969, pp. 185–95.
3. BARNA, Tibor. The interdependence of the British economy. *Journal of the Royal Statistical Society, Series A*, vol. CXV. pt. 1, 1952, pp. 29–81.
4. BARNA, Tibor (editor). *The Structural Interdependence of the Economy*, John Wiley, New York; A. Guiffrè, Milano; 1955.
5. BARNA, Tibor (editor). *Structural Interdependence and Economic Development*. Macmillan, London, 1963.
6. BERMAN, Lawrence. Flow of funds in the United Kingdom. *Journal of the Royal Statistical Society, Series A*, vol. 128, pt. 3, 1965, pp. 321–60.
7. BOWLEY, Arthur L., and Josiah STAMP. *The National Income 1924*. Clarendon Press, Oxford, 1927.
8. CAMBRIDGE, DEPARTMENT OF APPLIED ECONOMICS. *Exploring 1972, with Special Reference to the Balance of Payments*. No. 9 in *A Programme for Growth*. Chapman and Hall, London, 1970.
9. CAMBRIDGE, DEPARTMENT OF APPLIED ECONOMICS. *The Financial Interdependence of the Economy, 1957–1966*. No. 11 in *A Programme for Growth*. Chapman and Hall, London, 1971.
10. CARTER, A. P., and A. BRÓDY (editors). *Input-Output Analysis*. 2 vols., North-Holland Publishing Co., Amsterdam, 1970.

11. CARTER, C. F. Estimates of the gross domestic product of Northern Ireland, 1950–56. *Journal of the Statistical and Social Inquiry Society of Ireland*, vol. XX, pt. II, 1955–56, p. 149.

12. CARTER, C. F., and Mary ROBSON. A comparison of the national incomes and social accounts of Northern Ireland, the Republic of Ireland and the United Kingdom. *Journal of the Statistical and Social Inquiry Society of Ireland*, vol. XIX, 1954–55, pp. 62–87.

13. CHAMPERNOWNE, D. G. A model of income distribution. *The Economical Journal*, vol. LXIII, no. 250, 1953, pp. 318–51.

14. CHAMPERNOWNE, D. G. *Estimation and Uncertainty in Economics*. 3 vols., Oliver and Boyd, Edinburgh and London, 1969.

15. CHENERY, Hollis B., and Paul G. CLARK. *Interindustry Economics*. John Wiley, New York, 1959.

16. CONRAD, Alfred H., and John R. MEYER. *Studies in Econometric History*. Chapman and Hall, London, 1965.

17. COPELAND, Morris A. *A Study of Moneyflows in the United States*. National Bureau of Economic Research, New York, 1952.

18. DEANE, Phyllis. New estimates of gross national product for the United Kingdom, 1830–1914. *The Review of Income and Wealth*, series 14, no. 2, 1968, pp. 95–112.

19. FEINSTEIN, Charles. *National Income, Expenditure and Output of the United Kingdom, 1855–1965*. Cambridge University Press, 1972.

20. FISHER, Irving. *The Making of Index Numbers*. Houghton Mifflin Co., Boston and New York, third edition, 1927.

21. GEARY, R. C. A note on the comparison of exchange rates and purchasing power between countries. *Journal of the Royal Statistical Society, Series A*, vol. 121, pt. 1, 1958, pp. 97–9.

22. GIBRAT, R. *Les Inégalités Économiques*. Recueil Sirey, Paris, 1931.

23. Gilbert, Milton, and associates. *Comparative National Products and Price Levels.* O.E.E.C., Paris, 1958.
24. Goldsmith, Raymond W. *The National Wealth of the United States in the Postwar Period.* Princeton University Press, 1962.
25. Goldsmith, Raymond W., Robert E. Lipsey and Morris Mendelson. *Studies in the National Balance Sheet of the United States.* 2 vols., Princeton University Press, 1963.
26. Hicks, J. R. *The Social Framework.* The Clarendon Press, Oxford, 1942; second edition, 1952.
27. IJzeren, J. van. Three methods of comparing the purchasing power of currencies. Netherlands Central Bureau of Statistics, *Statistical Studies*, no. 7. W. de Haan N.V., Zeist, December 1956.
28. Leontief, Wassily W. Quantitative input and output relations in the economic system of the United States. *The Review of Economic Statistics*, vol. XVIII, no. 3, 1936, pp. 105–25.
29. Leontief, Wassily W. *The Structure of American Economy*. First edition (*1919–1929*), Harvard University Press, Cambridge, Mass, 1941; second edition (*1919–1939*), Oxford University Press, New York, 1951.
30. Lomax, K. S. Production and productivity movements in the United Kingdom since 1900. *Journal of the Royal Statistical Society*, *Series A*, vol. 122, pt. 2, 1959, pp. 185–220.
31. London and Cambridge Economic Service. *The British Economy: Key Statistics, 1900–1970*. Times Newspapers Ltd., London, 1971.
32. Lydall, H. F. *British Incomes and Savings*. Blackwell, Oxford, 1955.
33. McCrone, David. *Scotland's Economic Progress, 1951–1960*. Allen and Unwin, London, 1965.
34. Meade, J. E., and Richard Stone. *National Income and Expenditure*. Bowes and Bowes, London, fourth edition, 1957.

35. NETHERLANDS ECONOMIC INSTITUTE. *Input-Output Relations*. H. E. Stenfert Kroese N.V., Leiden, 1953.
36. NEVIN, Edward. *The Social Accounts of the Welsh Economy, 1948–56*. No. 2 in *Welsh Economic Studies*. University of Wales Press, Cardiff, 1957.
37. NEVIN, Edward, A. R. ROE and J. I. ROUND. *The Structure of the Welsh Economy*. No. 4 in *Welsh Economic Studies*. University of Wales Press, Cardiff, 1966.
38. O.E.C.D. *Main Economic Indicators*. O.E.C.D., Paris, monthly.
39. O.E.C.D. *National Accounts of O.E.C.D. countries, 1950–1968*. O.E.C.D., Paris, 1970.
40. O.E.C.D. *Seasonal Adjustment on Electronic Computers*. O.E.C.D., Paris, 1960.
41. O.E.E.C. *A Standardized System of National Accounts*. O.E.E.C., Paris, 1952; *1958 Edition*, 1959.
42. PAIGE, Deborah, and Gottfried BOMBACH. *A Comparison of National Output and Productivity of the United Kingdom and the United States*. O.E.E.C., Paris, 1959.
43. REVELL, Jack, and others. *The Wealth of the Nation*. Cambridge University Press, 1967.
44. STEWART, I. G. Input-output table for the United Kingdom, 1948. *The Times Review of Industry*, London and Cambridge Economic Bulletin, new series, no. 28, 1958, pp. vii-ix.
45. STONE, Richard. *Quantity and Price Indexes in National Accounts*. O.E.E.C., Paris, 1956.
46. STONE, Richard. *Input-Output and National Accounts*. O.E.E.C., Paris, 1961.
47. STONE, Richard. Social accounts at the regional level: a survey. In *Regional Economic Planning: Techniques of Analysis*; O.E.E.C., Paris, 1961. Reprinted in *Mathematics in the Social Sciences and Other Essays*; Chapman and Hall, London, 1966.
48. STONE, Richard. Demographic input-output: an extension of social accounting. In [10, vol. 1, pp. 293–319].

49. STONE, Richard. Input-output and demographic accounting: a tool for educational planning. *Minerva*, vol. IV, no. 3, 1966, pp. 365–80. Reprinted in [50].

50. STONE, Richard. *Mathematical Models of the Economy and Other Essays*. Chapman and Hall, London, 1970.

51. STONE, Richard. A system of social matrices. Paper presented to the Twelfth General Conference of the International Association for Research in Income and Wealth, Rönneby, 1971. Mimeographed.

52. STONE, Richard. *Demographic Accounting and Model Building*. O.E.C.D., Paris, 1971.

53. STONE, Richard. The fundamental matrix of the active sequence. Paper presented to the Fifth International Conference on Input-Output Techniques, Geneva, 1971. Mimeographed.

54. STONE, Richard and Giovanna, and Jane GUNTON. An example of demographic accounting: the school ages. *Minerva*, vol. VI, no. 2, 1968, pp. 185–212. Reprinted in [50].

55. STONE, Richard, and Giovanna CROFT-MURRAY. *Social Accounting and Economic Models*. Bowes and Bowes, London, 1959.

56. U.K., BANK OF ENGLAND. *Bank of England Quarterly Bulletin*. Bank of England, London, quarterly.

57. U.K., BOARD OF TRADE and CENTRAL STATISTICAL OFFICE. *Input-Output Tables for the United Kingdom, 1954*. Studies in Official Statistics, No. 8. H.M.S.O., London, 1961.

58. U.K., CENTRAL STATISTICAL OFFICE. *Abstract of Regional Statistics*. H.M.S.O., London, annually.

59. U.K., CENTRAL STATISTICAL OFFICE. *Annual Abstract of Statistics*. H.M.S.O., London, annually.

60. U.K., CENTRAL STATISTICAL OFFICE. *Economic Trends*. H.M.S.O., London, monthly.

61. U.K., CENTRAL STATISTICAL OFFICE. *National Income and Expenditure*. H.M.S.O., London, annually.

62. U.K., Central Statistical Office. *Preliminary Estimates of National Income and Balance of Payments.* H.M.S.O., London, annually.

63. U.K., Central Statistical Office. *United Kingdom Balance of Payments.* H.M.S.O., London, annually.

64. U.K., Central Statistical Office. *National Income Statistics: Sources and Methods.* H.M.S.O., London, 1956.

65. U.K., Central Statistical Office. *The Index of Industrial Production: Method of Compilation.* H.M.S.O., London, 1959.

66. U.K., Central Statistical Office. *National Accounts Statistics: Sources and Methods.* H.M.S.O., London, 1968.

67. U.K., Central Statistical Office. *Input-Output Tables for the United Kingdom, 1963.* Studies in Official Statistics, no. 16. H.M.S.O., London, 1970.

68. U.K., Committee on the Working of the Monetary System (Radcliffe Committee). *Report.* Cmnd. 827, H.M.S.O., London, 1959.

69. U.K., East Anglia Economic Planning Council. *East Anglia: a study.* H.M.S.O., London, 1968.

70. U.K., Government of Northern Ireland. *Digest of Statistics.* H.M.S.O., Belfast, half-yearly.

71. U.K., Inland Revenue. *Inland Revenue Statistics. 1970.* H.M.S.O., London, 1970.

72. U.K., Ministry of Labour. *Family Expenditure Survey.* H.M.S.O., London, annually.

73. U.K., Treasury. *Economic Report.* H.M.S.O., London, annually.

74. U.K., Treasury. *United Kingdom Balance of Payments 1946–1957.* H.M.S.O., London, 1959.

75. U.N., Department of Economic and Social Affairs, Statistical Office. *A System of National Accounts and Supporting Tables.* Studies in Methods, series F, no. 2, United Nations, New York, 1953; rev. 1, 1960; rev. 2, 1964.

76. U.N., Department of Economic and Social Affairs, Statistical Office. *A System of National Accounts.* Studies in Methods, series F, no. 2, rev. 3. United Nations, New York, 1968.

77. U.N., Department of Economic and Social Affairs, Statistical Office. *Yearbook of National Accounts Statistics.* United Nations, New York, annually since 1957.

78. U.N., Economic and Social Council, Statistical Commission. *Basic Methodological Rules for the Compilation of the Statistical Balance of the National Economy.* E/CN.3/396, United Nations, New York, 1969. Mimeographed.

79. U.S., Board of Governors of the Federal Reserve System. *Federal Reserve Bulletin.* Board of Governors of the Federal Reserve System, Washington, monthly.

80. U.S., Board of Governors of the Federal Reserve System. *Flow of Funds in the United States 1939–1953.* Board of Governors of the Federal Reserve System, Washington, 1955.

81. U.S., Department of Commerce. *Survey of Current Business.* U.S. Government Printing Office, Washington, monthly.

82. U.S., Department of Commerce. *National Income, 1954 Edition.* U.S. Government Printing Office, Washington, 1954.

83. U.S., Department of Commerce. *U.S. Income and Output.* U.S. Government Printing Office, Washington, 1959.

84. U.S., Department of Commerce. *The National Income and Product Accounts of the United States, 1929–1965: Statistical Tables.* U.S. Government Printing Office, Washington, 1966.

85. U.S., Department of Commerce. *Income Distribution in the United States by Size, 1944–1950.* U.S. Government Printing Office, Washington, 1953.

86. U.S., Department of Commerce. *The Balance of Payments of the United States.* U.S. Government Printing Office, Washington, annually.
87. U.S., Department of Commerce. *Personal Income by States since 1929.* U.S. Government Printing Office, Washington, 1956.
88. U.S., Department of Commerce. *Long Term Economic Growth.* U.S. Government Printing Office, Washington, 1966.
89. Woodward, V. H. Regional social accounts for the United Kingdom. National Institute of Economic and Social Research, *Regional Papers I.* Cambridge University Press, 1970.